moda All-Stars

SCRAPS
MADE SIMPLE

*15 Sensationally Scrappy
Quilts from Precuts*

Compiled by Lissa Alexander

Martingale
Create with Confidence

DEDICATION

To the wonderfully diverse quilt shops around the world that help quilters accumulate a healthy stash of fabrics from which to create scrap quilts—we couldn't have done this without you, literally!

With special thanks to the incredibly talented designers who make Moda Fabrics look their best in all the projects they create.

All royalties for this book will be donated to Alzheimer's Association (alz.org), a nonprofit health organization dedicated to accelerating the progress of treating, preventing and curing Alzheimer's disease.

Scraps Made Simple:
15 Sensationally Scrappy Quilts from Precuts
© 2016 by Martingale & Company®

Martingale®
19021 120th Ave. NE, Ste. 102
Bothell, WA 98011-9511 USA
ShopMartingale.com

Printed in China
21 20 19 18 17 16   8 7 6 5 4 3 2

**Library of Congress Cataloging-in-Publication Data
is available upon request.**

ISBN: 978-1-60468-759-0

MISSION STATEMENT

We empower makers who use fabric and yarn to make life more enjoyable.

CREDITS

**PUBLISHER AND
CHIEF VISIONARY OFFICER**
Jennifer Erbe Keltner

CONTENT DIRECTOR
Karen Costello Soltys

DESIGN MANAGER
Adrienne Smitke

MANAGING EDITOR
Tina Cook

PRODUCTION MANAGER
Regina Girard

ACQUISITIONS EDITOR
Karen M. Burns

COVER DESIGNER
Adrienne Smitke

TECHNICAL EDITOR
Beth Bradley

INTERIOR DESIGNER
Connor Chin

COPY EDITOR
Sheila Chapman Ryan

PHOTOGRAPHER
Brent Kane

ILLUSTRATOR
Rose Wright

Contents

Introduction

If it's scrappy, we're happy! That could be the mantra of the all-star Moda designers featured in this book. For them, more is better when it comes to combining fabrics in a quilt. But don't fret if your stash or confidence isn't yet up to the task of making a spectacular scrappy quilt. The secret to scrappy success is quite possibly waiting for you rolled or wrapped in a precut bundle! Starting with Charm Packs, Layer Cakes, Jelly Rolls, fat eighths, and fat quarters, you can achieve the look you love with the expert advice of these seasoned quilters. And this book doesn't stop at fabulous quilt patterns from all-star quilters. No, it gives you insight into how they get the scrappy look they love, how they store their own scraps, and gobs of color advice too. The questions we asked each designer are below. You'll find their answers alongside each of their quilt projects. So every step of the way, you'll be learning more about the designers you love and increasing your own SK quotient (that's Scrap Knowledge). And if the wonderful world of precuts is still a bit of a mystery to you, turn the page and check out "A Primer on Precuts." Mystery solved! By the end of your first project, you'll agree scrappy is simple!

SCRAPS OF
Wisdom
WHAT WE ASKED

- A scrap that is (how small?) is not too small to save.

- In my dreams, the ideal scrappy quilt has at least ___ different fabrics in it.

- Let me tell you a little something about how I store my scraps. I _____ .

- When I start pulling fabrics for a scrappy quilt, I begin with/by . . . .

- If you look at my assortment of scraps, you'll see _____ is the most prominent color. The color you'll find the least of in my scraps is _____.

- The best advice I've given or received on choosing/mixing colors/prints for scrap quilts was _____.

- If I had a signature move, I'd say you'll know a quilt is mine by looking because . . . .

- Thumbs up or thumbs down? Scrappy binding? Scrappy backing?

- Here's my secret to keeping your ¼" seam allowances spot on: _____.

- One tip that will make creating my quilt easier/faster/more accurately is _____.

- These six things are given: sewing machine, fabric, thread, rotary mat/cutter/ruler. You can add three more things to your quilter's must-have list. What do you add?

A Primer on Precuts

You see them in bundles at your favorite quilt shop, tucked into artful displays. You admire them on the shelves or in bins in your friends' sewing rooms. But what exactly is included in those delightful bundles of fabrics? What's the difference between a Layer Cake and a Jelly Roll? These sweet treats (often known by their dessert-like names) are really sweets for the fabric-lover's soul. So brush up on your precut vocabulary with this quick primer. WARNING: It might just increase your appetite for more fabric!

Charm Pack. Think of a charm pack as the sampler platter of small desserts. A Charm Pack has forty-two 5" x 5" squares. Depending on how many designs are in a collection, there might be duplicates of some prints in a charm pack. But you're sure to get a little of everything in the collection when you pick up one of these. And here's a little secret, if you love having bits of it all, be on the lookout for Moda Candy (aka mini charms) that contain forty-two 2½" x 2½" squares. Finally, word to the wise—these are meant to be cut and sewn as is. No need to prewash these little treasures.

Layer Cake. With four times the appeal of a charm pack, a Layer Cake gives you 42 squares, each measuring 10" x 10". (See what we did there? You could cut four charm packs from a Layer Cake, thus four times the appeal.) Just like the charm pack, you may have several duplicate prints in a Layer Cake, depending on the number of prints in a collection. Fabric collectors be alert! Did you know, there's also a Junior Layer Cake? Hard to find, but fun when you do, a Junior has 20 squares total.

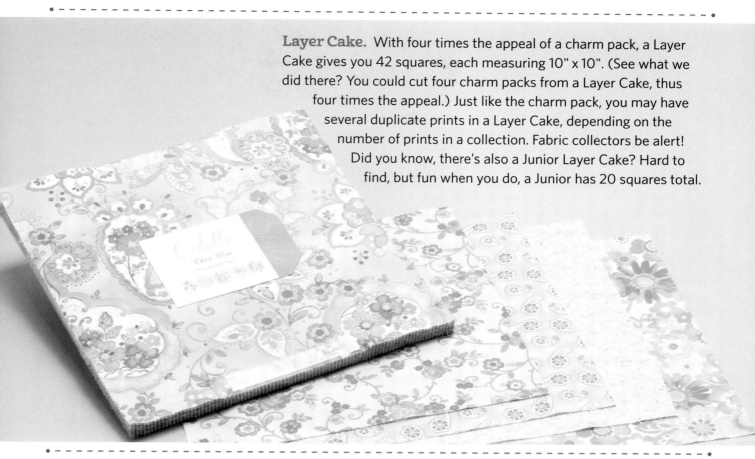

Jelly Roll. It's a bit racy, but the Jelly Roll has been known to appear at quilt shop strip clubs around the world! After all, who can resist the appeal of a chubby roll of forty 2½" x 44" fabric strips? Not us! This, for many quilters, is the precut that started their fabric lovin' hearts racing with possibilities. Plenty of patterns are designed around this special precut, and it's so (sew!) easy to get the scrappy look when you begin with a Jelly Roll. Most contain a single strip of each print in a collection. Don't even think about prewashing these beauties or you'll end up with a mop. They're just fine to use right out of the roll. P.S. A Junior Jelly Roll has 20 strips total.

Fat-Eighth Bundle. It's about to get serious here. No more strips and squares—we're talking more substantial pieces of fabric now. A fat-eighth bundle contains one of each print in a collection. So, the number of pieces in the bundle will vary depending of which fabric collection it contains. The fat-eighth bundle is really the little sister to the more well-known fat-quarter bundle. Here's the skinny—a fat eighth is 9" x 22" (shorter and wider than a standard ⅛-yard cut of 4½" x 44"). This is the Goldilocks of precut bundles for you if a Layer Cake is too small and a Fat Quarter bundle is too big.

Fat-Quarter Bundle. These bundles look awesome in your sewing room, even if you never untie the string! Just set them around and marvel at their beauty. The queen of all precuts, the fat quarter has been a big fat deal for as long as we can remember. The start of many a quilter's stash begins with this specially cut quarter yard of fabric. What makes it fat? A standard quarter-yard cut would be a 9" x 44" strip. Each fat quarter is 18" x 22", which allows you to cut more shapes and sizes, especially helpful if you're cutting larger geometric pieces or appliqué shapes. A fat-quarter bundle contains one of every print in a collection. So the number of pieces varies depending on which collection you're buying.

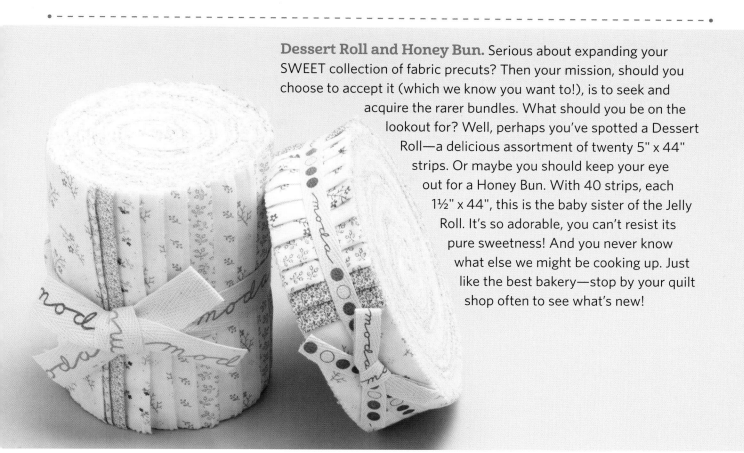

Dessert Roll and Honey Bun. Serious about expanding your SWEET collection of fabric precuts? Then your mission, should you choose to accept it (which we know you want to!), is to seek and acquire the rarer bundles. What should you be on the lookout for? Well, perhaps you've spotted a Dessert Roll—a delicious assortment of twenty 5" x 44" strips. Or maybe you should keep your eye out for a Honey Bun. With 40 strips, each 1½" x 44", this is the baby sister of the Jelly Roll. It's so adorable, you can't resist its pure sweetness! And you never know what else we might be cooking up. Just like the best bakery—stop by your quilt shop often to see what's new!

A Solid Idea. Everyone knows prints are charming, but every now and then you want a setting square or solid sashing and you'd rather limit your time spent cutting them from yardage. Have no fear! Bella Solids are here and available in a variety of precut shapes and sizes.

Designed by Carrie Nelson; quilted by Diane Tricka

Old School

Use as many different fabrics as you have on hand to make this super scrappy quilt that consists of just one fun and simple block.

Finished quilt: 71¾" x 76¾"
Finished block: 5" x 5"

Materials

Yardage is based on 42"-wide fabric.

⅓ yard *each* of 15 assorted light prints OR scraps of as many light prints desired to total 225 squares, 4½" x 4½"*

⅓ yard *each* of 29 assorted medium/dark prints OR scraps of as many medium/dark prints desired to total 225 rectangles, 4½" x 10"*

¾ yard of pink stripe for binding

4½ yards of backing fabric

80" x 85" piece of batting

1¼" finished triangle piecing paper such as Primitive Gatherings or Spinning Stars (optional)

* Incorporate precut 5" x 5" charm squares or 5" x 42" strips if desired.

Cutting

All measurements include ¼"-wide seam allowances.

From the assorted light prints, cut:
225 squares, 4½" x 4½"

From the assorted medium/dark prints, cut *210 matching pairs* of small and large squares:
1 square, 4½" x 4½" (210 total)
1 square, 4¼" x 4¼" (210 total)

From the remaining assorted medium/dark prints, cut:
15 squares, 4½" x 4½"

From the pink stripe, cut:
8 strips, 2" x 42"*

Carrie used 2"-wide strips for a skinny binding that complements the intricate quilt design, but you can cut 2½"-wide strips if you prefer a slightly wider binding.

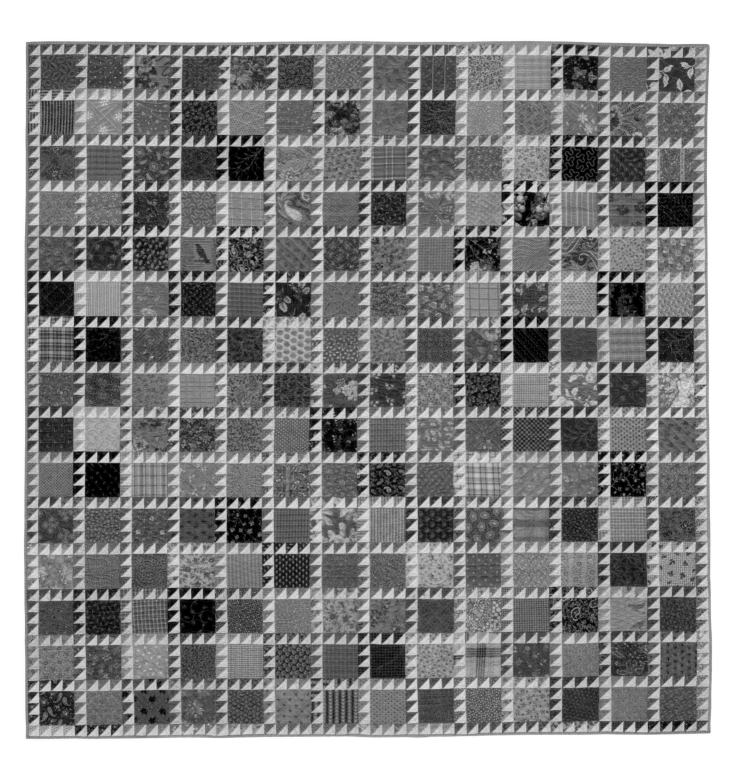

Assembling the Blocks

The quilt consists of 210 blocks set in 15 rows of 14 blocks each, plus rows of half-square-triangle units to finish the right side and bottom edge of the quilt. Each block is made using one light square and one matching set of medium/dark 4½" and 4¼" squares.

Simple Sizing

Because this quilt is made from only one repeat block, it's easy to customize the finished quilt to the size you want. After you've decided the quilt size you'd like to make, determine how many 5" x 5" blocks are needed to achieve those measurements.

1 If desired, use 1¼" triangle piecing paper to make the half-square-triangle units, or use the following method. Place one light and one medium/dark 4½" square right sides together. On the wrong side of the light square, draw two intersecting diagonal lines from corner to corner as shown. Using a scant ¼" seam allowance, stitch on both sides of each line.

2 Cut the stitched square into quarters, and then cut each quarter along the drawn diagonal line to yield eight half-square-triangle units. Press the seam allowances toward the dark fabric, and then trim each unit to measure 1¾" x 1¾".

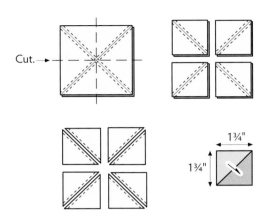

3 Lay out seven of the half-square-triangle units along the left and top edge of the matching medium/dark 4¼" square as shown. (One half-square-triangle unit is extra). Join the four top half-square-triangle units into one row and the three side units into one column. Press the seam allowances in one direction.

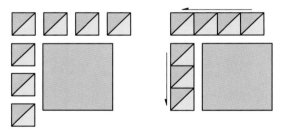

Carrie is a certified scrapaholic known to travel the country in search of a fabric fix and having little trouble finding one, or more! Visit blog.ModaFabrics.com.

- **A scrap that is** 1" x 3" is not too small for me to save. It really depends on what future projects I know I have living in my head.

- **In my dreams, the ideal scrappy quilt has at least** 100 different fabrics in it. But that really isn't required. In the past year, I've made several scrap quilts that I love that have fewer than 50.

- **Let me tell you a little something about how I store my scraps.** Store my scraps? I'm supposed to store them? That sounds a little bit like organizing them. Baskets and bins, mostly by color, sometimes by type (repros, designer, etc.).

- **When I start pulling fabrics for a scrappy quilt,** I begin with not much of a plan. Most often it's a "feel" for how I want the finished quilt to look.

- **If you look at my assortment of scraps, you'll see** red is the most prominent color. **The colors you'll find the least of in my scraps are** purple and burgundy.

- **If I had a signature move, I'd say you'll know a quilt is mine by looking because** it would have a pieced border or no border, and a contrast narrow binding.

- **Thumbs up or thumbs down? Scrappy binding?** Thumbs UP!! **Scrappy backing?** Thumbs UP!!

- **One little tip that will make creating MY quilt easier is** if you think all the points in this quilt are perfect, you're not looking closely enough!

---

4 Sew the half-square-triangle column to the left side of the square; press the seam allowances toward the square. Sew the half-square-triangle row to the top edge of the block. Press the seam allowances toward the square. Clip the seam allowances at the square-corner intersection if needed in order to smoothly press. The block should measure 5½" square, including seam allowances. Make 210 blocks.

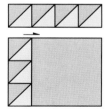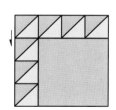

Make 210.

Assembling the Border Strips

1 From the remaining light and medium/dark 4½" squares, make 15 sets of half-square-triangle units measuring 1¾" x 1¾". Use the method from "Assembling the Blocks" on page 12 to make eight half-square-triangle units at once, and then divide the units into 29 matching sets of four. (One set of four half-square-triangle units will be extra).

2 Select 15 sets of half-square-triangle units for the side border strips. Join the units in each set as shown. Join the remaining 14 sets of half-square-triangle units as shown for the bottom border strips. Press the seam allowances in one direction.

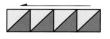

Make 15 side strips.   Make 14 bottom strips.

Assembling the Quilt Top

1 Lay out 15 rows of 14 blocks each. Place the border strips along the right side and the bottom edge as shown. Place one of the extra remaining half-square triangles in the lower-right corner.

2 Join the blocks and side border strips in each row, pressing the seam allowances in alternating directions from row to row. Join the bottom border strips and corner half-square-triangle unit. Join the rows and bottom border strip; press the seam allowances in one direction.

Finishing the Quilt

For more details on quilting and finishing, go to ShopMartingale.com/HowtoQuilt.

1 Layer the backing, batting, and quilt top; baste the layers together. Hand or machine quilt as desired. Carrie's quilt features a loop design in the half-square-triangle sections and a sampling of different motifs and designs—including stars, feathers, flowers, and crosshatching—in each individual square.

2 Use the pink-stripe 2"-wide strips to make and attach the binding.

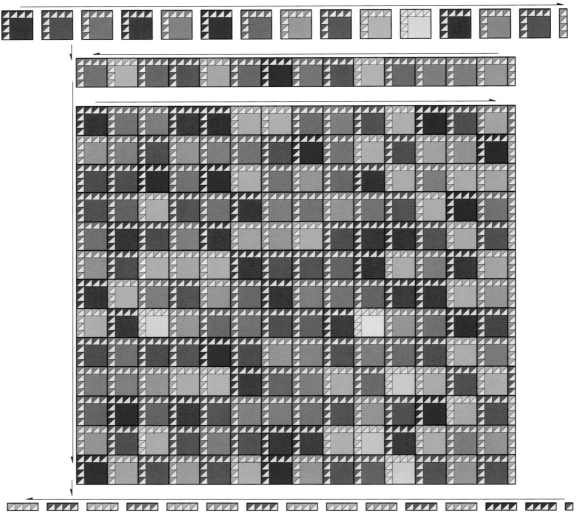

Quilt assembly

"Embrace Wabi-Sabi—the Japanese art of finding beauty in imperfection."

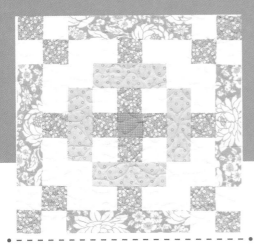

Scrap Basket Quilt

Precut 2½"-wide strips make the piecing for these oversized blocks extra speedy. Mix bright red, blue, green, and yellow prints with a fresh white background for a graphic look.

Finished quilt: 62½" x 82½"
Finished block: 18" x 18"

Materials

Yardage is based on 42"-wide fabric. Measure precut strips prior to cutting to ensure they're at least 42" wide, or if you're using scraps, measure to ensure the total length is at least 42".

1 Jelly Roll of 40 white strips, 2½" x 42", OR 3⅛ yards of white solid cut into 40 strips, 2½"-wide, for blocks and sashing

36 assorted print strips, 2½" x 42", for blocks

⅝ yard of red print for binding

5 yards of backing fabric

68" x 92" piece of batting

Cutting

All measurements include ¼"-wide seam allowances. The quilt consists of 12 blocks; each block requires two white strips and three assorted print strips (labeled A, B, and C). Plan the color combinations and placement for each block before cutting.

Cutting for 1 Block
From 2 white strips, cut:
1 strip, 2½" x 21½"
2 strips, 2½" x 10½"
8 rectangles, 2½" x 4½"
From the A strip, cut:
1 strip, 2½" x 21½"
1 strip, 2½" x 10½"
4 squares, 2½" x 2½"
From the B strip, cut:
4 strips, 2½" x 6½"
From the C strip, cut:
4 strips, 2½" x 10½"

Continued on page 18

Continued from page 16

Cutting for Sashing, Block Centers, and Binding

From the remainders of the assorted print strips, cut:

32 squares, 2½" x 2½"

From the remaining 16 white strips, cut:

31 strips, 2½" x 18½"

From the red print, cut:

8 strips, 2½" x 42"

Assembling the Blocks

After cutting, sort the fabrics for each block. You'll need one set of white background pieces, one set of A pieces, one set of B strips, and one set of C strips. Select a 2½" center square in a color similar to fabric C, cut from the print-strip leftovers.

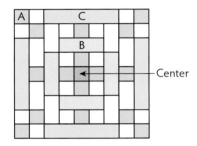

1 Sew one A and two white 2½" x 10½" strips as shown. Press the seam allowances toward the A strip. Crosscut the strip unit into four sections, each 2½" x 6½".

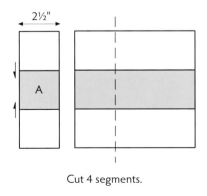

Cut 4 segments.

2 Sew the center square between two A squares. Press the seam allowances toward the A squares.

3 Sew the center unit between two strip sections from step 1 to create a 6½" square nine-patch unit. Press seam allowances toward the center row.

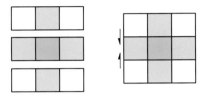

4 Sew B strips to the top and bottom of the nine-patch unit. Sew the two remaining strip sections from step 1 to the top and bottom of the unit. Press the seam allowances toward the B strips.

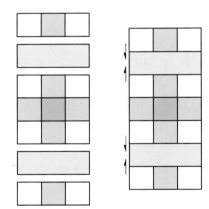

5 Sew white 2½" x 4½" rectangles to both ends of two remaining B strips. Press seam allowances toward the B strips. Sew these 2½" x 14½" strip units to the sides of the block as shown. Press the seam allowances toward the units just added.

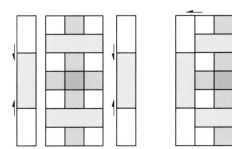

SCRAPS OF
Wisdom
FROM AMY SMART

Amy is Director of Scraps in her sewing room, leaving no small scraps behind. Visit DiaryofaQuilter.com.

- **A scrap that is** 1½" square is not too small to save.

- **In my dreams, the ideal scrappy quilt has at least** 50 different fabrics in it.

- **If you look at my assortment of scraps, you'll see** red is the most prominent color. **The color you'll find the least of in my scraps is** purple.

- **Thumbs up or thumbs down? Scrappy binding?** I love a binding that has a few surprises. **Scrappy backing?** I love pieced backs! They're a great way to bust through my stash and a chance to make another quilt, in a way.

- **Let me tell you a little something about how I store my scraps.** I sort almost all my scraps by color,

although I do have a separate container of 2½" strips of all colors. The rest go directly into clear plastic drawers by color. I feel much more inspired to use them when they're separated by color. I've also started to purge my scraps on a regular basis. There's nothing less inspiring than fabric you don't love anymore.

- **When I start pulling fabrics for a scrappy quilt,** I first find a color palette that inspires me—whether it's by looking at pictures of antique quilts or color stories on Pinterest, or Design Seeds. Then, I pull as many fabrics as possible from my scraps that fit in that range.

- **Here's my secret to keeping your ¼" seam allowances spot on:** Sew with a scant ¼". I set my needle over one spot on my machine, and using a regular presser foot as a guide, I get a perfect scant ¼".

6 Sew C strips to the top and bottom edges of the block. Press the seam allowances toward the C strips. The unit should be 10½" x 18½".

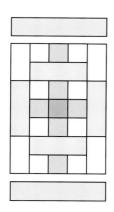
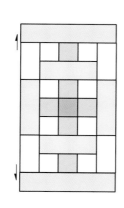

7 Sew one A square between two white 2½" x 4½" rectangles. Press the seam allowances toward the square. Sew a C strip to one long edge of the unit. Press the seam allowances toward the C strip. Make two. The units should be 10½" x 4½".

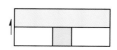

Make 2.

8 Sew together the white and A 2½" x 21½" strips. Press the seam allowance toward the A strip. Crosscut the strip unit into eight sections, 2½" wide. Assemble the units in pairs to make four-patch units that measure 4½" square, including seam allowances. Press the seam allowances in one direction.

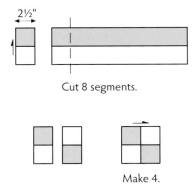

Cut 8 segments.

Make 4.

9 Sew four-patch units to both ends of the strip units from step 7. Press the seam allowances toward the strip units.

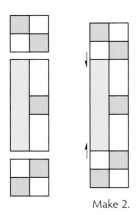

Make 2.

10 Sew the units from step 9 to the sides of the block. Press the seam allowances toward the center of the block. Make 12 blocks that are 18½" square, including seam allowances.

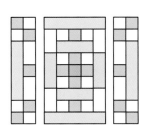 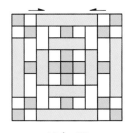

Make 12.

Assembling the Quilt Top

1 Lay out four rows of three blocks, alternating the blocks with white 2½" x 18½" strips as shown. Join the blocks and white strips. Press the seam allowances toward the blocks. Sew five horizontal sashing strips by alternating four print 2½" squares with three white 2½" x 18½" strips. Press the seam allowances toward the squares. Arrange the four rows and five sashing strips as shown.

Quilt assembly

2 Join the sashing strips and block rows. Press the seam allowances toward the sashing strips.

Finishing the Quilt

For more details on quilting and finishing, go to ShopMartingale.com/HowtoQuilt.

1 Layer the backing, batting, and quilt top; baste the layers together. Hand or machine quilt as desired. Amy chose an allover quilting pattern of daisies, a playful complement to the many geometric shapes in the quilt.

2 Use the red 2½"-wide strips to make and attach the binding.

"I started a scrap exchange with friends. When we get together occasionally to sew, we bring our scraps and we each have fun picking through the pile of new-to-us scraps!"

Designed by Laura Boehnke; quilted by Susan Urich

Chain Log Cabin

Strip piecing makes the blocks for this dramatic design much simpler than they look. Play up the patriotic look of stars and stripes by using scraps of red, cream, and blue batiks.

Finished quilt: 72½" x 90½"
Finished block: 9" x 9"

Materials

Yardage is based on 42"-wide fabric.

12 fat quarters OR 3 yards *total* of assorted blue prints for blocks and border 3*

11 fat quarters OR 2¾ yards *total* of assorted cream prints for blocks and border 2*

9 fat quarters OR 2¼ yards *total* of assorted black prints for blocks and border 4*

6 fat quarters OR 1⅜ yards *total* of assorted red prints for blocks*

1⅛ yards of black tone on tone for border 1 and binding

⅓ yard of red print for mock piping

5½ yards of backing fabric

79" x 97" piece of batting

This is the minimum number of fat quarters needed. Use more for a scrappier look if desired.

Cutting

All measurements include ¼"-wide seam allowances.

From the assorted black prints, cut:

48 strips, 1½" x 21"

4½"-wide strips of various lengths (cut from the remainder to equal 325" of length) for border 4

From the assorted red prints, cut:

28 strips, 1½" x 21"

384 squares, 1½" x 1½"

From the assorted cream prints, cut:

8 strips, 1½" x 21"

32 strips, 2½" x 21"

4 strips, 3½" x 21"

8 strips, 4½" x 21"

2"-wide strips of various lengths (cut from the remainder to equal 285" of length) for border 2

Continued on page 24

Continued from page 22

From the assorted blue prints, cut:

8 strips, 1½" x 21"

32 strips, 2½" x 21"

4 strips, 3½" x 21"

8 strips, 4½" x 21"

3"-wide strips of various lengths (cut from the remainder to equal 300" of length) for border 3

From the black tone on tone, cut:

8 strips, 1½" x 42"

9 strips, 2½" x 42"

From the red print, cut:

8 strips, 1¼" x 42"

Assembling the Center Squares

1 Sew red, blue, and cream 1½" x 21" strips together to make a blue/red/cream strip set. Make four. Press the seam allowances toward the red strips. Crosscut each strip unit into 12 segments, 1½" wide, for a total of 48 center segments.

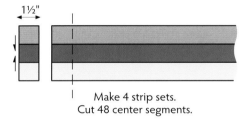

Make 4 strip sets.
Cut 48 center segments.

2 Sew a red 1½" x 21" strip to a blue 2½" x 21" strip. Press the seam allowances toward the red strips. Make four red/blue strip sets. Crosscut each strip set into 12 segments, 1½" wide, for a total of 48 red/blue segments. Repeat the process with red

and cream strips to make 48 red/cream segments; press the seam allowances toward the red strips.

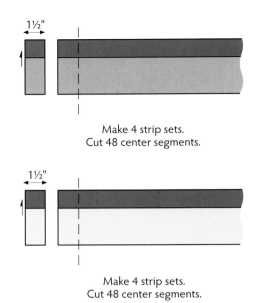

Make 4 strip sets.
Cut 48 center segments.

Make 4 strip sets.
Cut 48 center segments.

3 Sew one center segment between one red/blue segment and one red/cream segment as shown to make a block center. Press the seam allowances toward the center segment. Make 48 block centers that are 3½" square, including seam allowances.

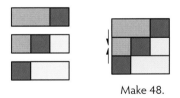

Make 48.

Assembling the Blocks

1 Sew a black 1½" x 21" strip to a blue 2½" x 21" strip to make a black/blue strip set. Repeat to make 20. Press the seam allowances toward the black strips. Crosscut *four* of the strip units into 12 segments, 1½" wide, for a total of 48 black/blue segments. Repeat with black and cream strips to

SCRAPS OF *Wisdom*
FROM LAURA BOEHNKE

Laura is a licensed scraptitioner, and her joy in sewing little bits of fabric together to make beautiful quilts is apparent in almost every quilt she completes.

- **A scrap or strip that is** 1" wide is not too small to save.

- **In my dreams, the ideal scrappy quilt has at least** 100+ (too many to count) fabrics in it!

- **Let me tell you a little something about how I store my scraps.** I separate the fabric by size of pieces. I like using old shoeboxes for strips and scraps. I use cube drawers to store fabric by color. All sizes of yardage can be placed in drawers for easy access.

- **When I start pulling fabrics for a scrappy quilt,** I begin by deciding what colors to use.

- **If you look at my assortment of scraps, you'll see** blue, green, and red are the most prominent colors. **The color you'll find the least of in my scraps is** pink.

- **The best advice I've received on choosing colors/ prints for scrap quilts was** to not have all your color choices matched perfectly. Put a few "ugly" fabrics in the mix. They add sparkle and character to the quilt.

- **If I had a signature move, I'd say you'll know a quilt is mine by looking because** it has a lot of piecing. I love working on a quilt with many small pieces.

- **Thumbs up or thumbs down? Scrappy binding?** Thumbs down. **Scrappy backing?** Thumbs up.

- **Here's my secret to keeping your ¼" seam allowances spot on:** Use a presser foot that has an accurate ¼" measurement and have both hands available to guide the fabric and make adjustments as you sew.

make 20 strip sets; cut four of the strip sets into 48 black/cream segments. Reserve the remaining strip sets.

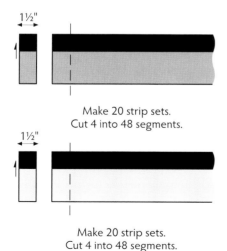

Make 20 strip sets.
Cut 4 into 48 segments.

Make 20 strip sets.
Cut 4 into 48 segments.

2 Sew a center square between one black/blue segment and one black/cream segment as shown. Press the seam allowances outward. Repeat to make 48 center rectangles that are 3½" x 5½", including seam allowances.

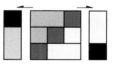

Make 48.

3 Sew four of the reserved black/blue strip sets between cream and red 1½ x 21" strips to make four strip sets as shown on page 26. Press the seam allowances toward the center. Crosscut each strip unit into 12 segments, 1½" wide, for a total of 48 blue-pieced segments. Repeat the process with four reserved black/cream strip sets, sewing

them between blue and red strips as shown to make 48 segments.

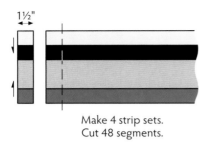

1½"

Make 4 strip sets.
Cut 48 segments.

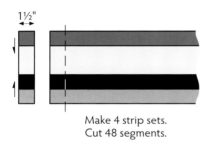

1½"

Make 4 strip sets.
Cut 48 segments.

4 Sew one *each* of the segments from step 3 to a center rectangle as shown to make a 5½" square center unit; press. Repeat to make 48 center units.

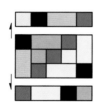

Make 48.

5 Sew a black 1½" x 21" strip, a cream 2½" x 21" strip, and a blue 2½" x 21" strip together as shown; make eight. Press the seam allowances toward the black strips. Crosscut each strip set into 12 segments, 1½" wide, for a total of 96 cream/black/blue segments.

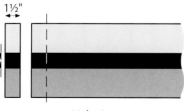

1½"

Make 8 strip sets.
Cut 96 segments.

6 Sew two cream/black/blue segments to opposite sides of a center unit as shown. Press the seam allowances away from center unit. Make 48 units that are 5½" x 7½", including seam allowances .

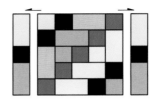

Make 48.

7 Sew one reserved black/blue strip unit between a cream 3½" x 21" strip and a red 1½" x 21" strip as shown. Press the seam allowances toward the black/blue strips. Make four strip sets. Crosscut each strip set into 12 segments, 1½" wide, for a total of 48 segments. Repeat the process with four reserved black/cream strip sets, sewing them between blue and red strips as shown to make 48 segments.

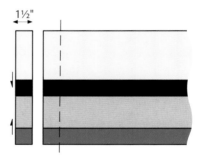

1½"

Make 4 strip sets.
Cut 48 segments.

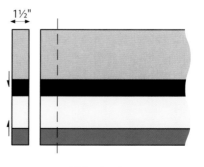

1½"

Make 4 strip sets.
Cut 48 segments.

8 Sew one *each* of the segments from step 7 to a center unit as shown; press. The block should now measure 7½" square. Make 48.

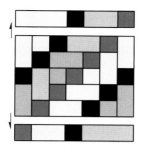

Make 48.

9 Sew cream 4½" x 21" strips to eight of the reserved black/blue strip sets as shown. Press the seam allowances toward the black strips. Crosscut each strip set into 12 segments, 1½" wide, for a total of 96 segments. Repeat the process to sew blue 4½" x 21" strips to eight of the reserved black/cream strip sets as shown and cut 96 segments.

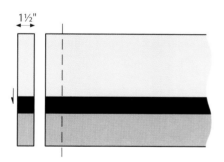

1½"

Make 8 strip sets.
Cut 96 segments.

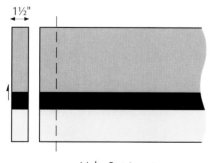

1½"

Make 8 strip sets.
Cut 96 segments.

10 Draw a diagonal line from corner to corner on the wrong side of 192 of the red 1½" squares. Place one marked square on the end of one long cream segment from step 9 as shown. Sew on the marked line, being careful to stitch across the correct diagonal. Trim the seam allowances to ¼" and press the square away from the pieced segment. Make 48 of unit A. Repeat the process with the long blue segments from step 9 to make 48 of unit B.

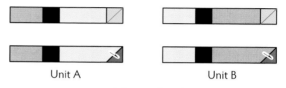

Unit A   Unit B

Make 48 of each.

11 Repeat step 10, but rotate the orientation of the marked line as shown. Make 48 each of units C and D.

Unit C   Unit D

Make 48 of each.

12 Sew red 1½" squares to both ends of 48 C units as shown. Press the seam allowances toward the red squares. Repeat to sew red squares to 48 D units as shown.

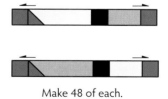

Make 48 of each.

13 Sew A and B units to opposite sides of a block as shown. Press the seam allowances toward the blocks. Sew C and D units to the top and bottom of the block as shown. Press the seam allowances toward the segments just added. The finished block should measure 9½" square, including seam allowances. Make 48 blocks.

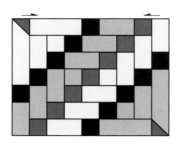

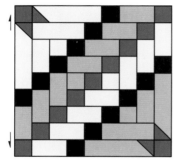

Make 48.

Assembling the Quilt Top

1 Arrange the blocks in eight rows of six blocks, rotating the blocks as shown in the quilt assembly diagram at right to create the pattern.

> *To speed up the process, use chain piecing as much as possible and layer the pieced strips with precision when cutting the sections in multiples.*

2 Join the blocks in each row. Press the seam allowances in alternating directions from row to row. Join the rows, and then press the seam allowances in one direction. The quilt top should now measure 54½" x 72½".

Quilt assembly

Adding the Borders

1 Border 1 is the innermost border. Join and trim the black tone-on-tone 1½"-wide strips to make top and bottom border strips measuring 1½" x 56½" and two side border strips measuring 1½" x 72½". Sew the side border strips to the sides of the quilt top; press the seam allowances toward the strips. Sew the top and bottom border strips to the top and bottom of the quilt; press. The quilt should now measure 56½" x 74½".

2 Border 2 is made from cream strips. Join and trim the cream 2"-wide strips to make top and bottom border strips measuring 2" x 59½" and two side border strips measuring 2" x 74½". Sew to the quilt top in the same manner as step 1; press. The quilt should now measure 59½" x 77½".

3 Border 3 is made from blue strips. Join and trim the blue 3"-wide strips to make top and bottom border strips measuring 3" x 64½" and two side border strips measuring 3" x 77½". Sew to the quilt top in the same manner as step 1; press. The quilt should now measure 64½" x 82½".

4 Border 4 is made from assorted black strips. Join and trim the black 4½"-wide strips to make top and bottom border strips measuring 4½" x 72½" and two side border strips measuring 4½" x 82½". Sew to the quilt top in the same manner as step 1; press. The quilt should now measure 72½" x 90½".

Finishing the Quilt

For more details on quilting and finishing, go to ShopMartingale.com/HowtoQuilt.

1 Layer the backing, batting, and quilt top; baste the layers together. Hand or machine quilt as desired. The featured quilt is machine quilted in a diagonal grid pattern to emphasize the diamond design. The quilting design also includes channel quilting and stars in the borders.

2 Use the red 1¼"-wide strips to make mock piping. Join and trim the strips to make two top and bottom strips measuring 1¼" x 72½" and two side strips measuring 1¼" x 90½". Fold each strip in half lengthwise with wrong sides together; press.

3 Place the top and bottom piping strips on the top and bottom edges of the quilt and place the side strips on the sides of the quilt, aligning the raw edges; pin. Baste the piping in place using a scant ¼" seam allowance. Press flat.

4 Use the black tone-on-tone 2½"-wide strips to make and attach the binding.

Housewarming

Stitch a neighborhood of sweet and scrappy houses. Choose the color combinations for the blocks as you cut so you can create perfect pairings for each house.

Finished quilt: 60½" x 76½"
Finished block: 10" x 10"

Materials

Yardage is based on 42"-wide fabric unless otherwise specified.
Fat eighths measure 9" x 21".

15 fat eighths of assorted floral prints for houses

24 strips, 2½" x 42", of assorted prints (12 light and 12 dark) for Four Patch blocks

8 fat eighths of assorted bright tone on tones for houses

1¼ yards of gray tone on tone for roofs and welcome mats

1 yard of aqua tone on tone for sky

3 fat eighths of assorted cream tone on tones for doors and windows

3 fat eighths of assorted green prints for grass

⅝ yard of multicolored print for binding

4 yards of backing fabric

67" x 83" piece of batting

Shades of Gray

If you want scrappier roofs, you can use three assorted gray tone on tones for the roof and sidewalk pieces in your quilt (as in the photo on page 31). Note that each block requires a matching set of two roof rectangles and one sidewalk rectangle. You'll need ½ yard of each print. Cut 10 sets of roof and sidewalk pieces from each print.

Cutting

All measurements include ¼"-wide seam allowances. You'll be able to cut the floral pieces for two houses from each of the 15 floral fat eighths.

Cutting for 1 House Block

From the floral prints, cut:
2 squares, 1¾" x 1¾"
4 rectangles, 1¾" x 3⅞"
4 rectangles, 1⅜" x 2⅛"
1 square, 4½" x 4½"

Continued on page 32

Continued from page 30

From the bright tone on tone, cut:

1 rectangle, 1¾" x 3¾"

2 rectangles, 1⅜" x 3⅜"

2 rectangles, 1½" x 5"

From the cream tone on tone, cut:

1 rectangle, 2" x 3⅜"

2 squares, 2⅛" x 2⅛"

From the aqua tone on tone, cut:

2 rectangles, 1¾" x 2⅛"

1 rectangle, 1¾" x 4¾"

2 rectangles, 3½" x 5"; cut them in half diagonally in opposite directions (top left to bottom right and top right to bottom left). You'll need 1 of each triangle for the block. Save the 2 leftover triangles for another block.

From the gray tone on tone, cut;

2 rectangles, 3½" x 6½"

1 rectangle, 1¾" x 2"

From the green print, cut:

2 rectangles, 1¾" x 4¾"

Cutting for Binding

From the multicolored print for binding, cut:

7 strips, 2½" x 42"

Assembling the House Blocks

Sewing each block individually allows you to see immediate progress, and it's easy to sew a block or two in your free time. If you prefer to chain piece, sew one block all the way through and look for opportunities to chain piece within the block.

1 Sew matching floral 1⅜" x 2⅛" rectangles to both sides of two matching cream 2⅛" squares. Press the seam allowances toward the rectangles. The unit should be 3⅞" x 2⅛", including seam allowances.

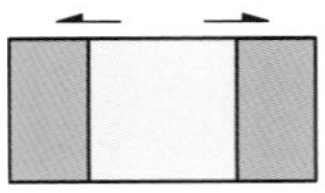

Make 2.

2 Sew matching 1¾" x 3⅞" floral rectangles to the top and bottom of the pieced units to create two window units that are 4⅝" x 3⅞", including seam allowances. Press the seam allowances toward the center.

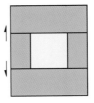

Make 2.

3 Sew matching bright 1⅜" x 3⅜" rectangles to the sides of one matching cream 2" x 3⅜" rectangle. Sew a matching bright 1¾" x 3¾" rectangle to the top of the pieced unit to create the door unit that is 3¾" x 4⅝", including seam allowances. Press all seam allowances toward the bright rectangles.

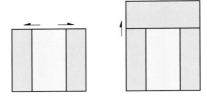

4 Sew the window units to the sides of the door unit, nesting the seam allowances. Press the seam allowances toward the window units. Sew a gray 1¾" x 2" rectangle between two matching green 1¾" x 4¾" rectangles to create a grass unit that is 1¾" x 10½", including seam allowances. Press the seam allowances toward the gray rectangle. Sew the grass unit to the bottom of the window/door unit. Press the seam allowances toward the grass unit.

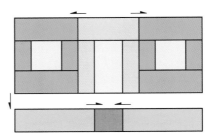

5 Sew aqua 1¾" x 2⅛" rectangles to one side of two matching floral 1¾" x 1¾" squares as shown.

SCRAPS OF
Wisdom
FROM AMY ELLIS

Amy is an interior scrap-orator using her artful arrangements of scraps to add beauty to otherwise ordinary rooms. Visit AmysCreativeSide.com.

- **A scrap that is** 2" square is not too small to save.

- **In my dreams, the ideal scrappy quilt has at least** 35 different fabrics in it.

- **Let me tell you a little something about how I store my scraps.** I like to collect scraps in one bin under my cutting table for a month or so, then sort by color into clear containers. This way, the scraps are beautiful and inspiring to look at in my sewing space.

- **When I start pulling fabrics for a scrappy quilt,** I begin by pulling one or two inspiration pieces of fabrics that I will work around for a cohesive quilt.

- **If you look at my assortment of scraps, you'll see** gray is the most prominent color. **The color you'll find the least of in my scraps is** orange.

- **The best advice I've given on choosing colors/prints for scrap quilts was** to pull everything that you like, then narrow the focus by using one or two main pieces to direct your selections.

- **Thumbs up or thumbs down? Scrappy binding?** Thumbs up. **Scrappy backing?** Thumbs up.

- **Here's my secret to keeping your ¼" seam allowances spot on:** I like to check my seam allowance often. Even small changes in thread can make a difference. Sew two pieces together and measure the outcome!

Press seam allowances toward floral squares. Sew these units to opposite ends of an aqua 1¾" x 4¾" rectangle to make a sky unit that is 1¾" x 10½", including seam allowances; press.

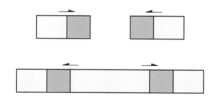

6 Make a copy of the paper-piecing pattern pieces on page 36. Cut out and join the pieces along the center dotted line. To make the roof unit, make 30 copies of the completed pattern. If needed, download free paper-foundation piecing instructions at ShopMartingale.com/HowtoQuilt. Paper piece the roof unit as follows, beginning on the left: use an aqua triangle for area 1; a gray 3½" x 6½" rectangle for area 2; a matching bright 1¾" x 5" rectangle for area 3; a matching floral 4½" square for area 4; another matching bright rectangle for area 5; another gray rectangle for area

6; and an aqua reversed triangle for area 7. Trim the edges of the unit along the outer dashed lines.

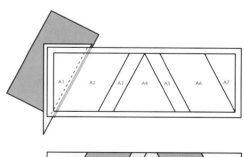

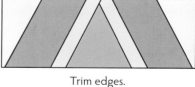

Trim edges.

" Add-a-Quarter ruler is my favorite tool for paper piecing. It makes trimming quick and perfect every time. "

7 Sew the roof unit to the top of the window/door unit. Press the seam allowances away from the roof. Sew the sky unit to the top of the roof unit. Press the seam allowances toward the sky unit to complete the House block. Make 30 House blocks that are 10½" square, including seam allowances.

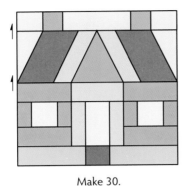

Make 30.

Assembling the Four Patch Blocks

1 Sew together one light and one dark 2½" x 42" strip. Press the seam allowances toward the dark strip. Make 12 strip sets. Crosscut the strip sets into 186 segments, 2½" wide.

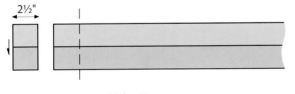

Make 12 strip sets.
Cut 186 segments.

2 Sew two segments together, placing the light and dark squares opposite each other as shown and nesting the seam allowances. Six segments will be extra; set them aside for now. Make 90 Four Patch blocks that are 4½" square, including seam allowances.

Make 90.

Assembling the Quilt Top

1 Lay out five rows of six House blocks each, distributing the variety of colors and prints in a pleasing arrangement.

2 Lay out six rows of 15 Four Patch blocks between the House rows as shown in the quilt assembly diagram on page 35.

3 Join the blocks in each row. Press the seam allowances in alternating directions from row to row. Each row should be 60½" wide.

4 Measure the length of your House block rows and use this measurement as a guide to adjust, if necessary, the Four Patch block rows. If needed, add the extra Four Patch segments to the ends of the Four Patch rows to equal the length of the House Rows. If your Four Patch rows are too long, trim an equal amount from each end so they're the same length as your House rows.

5 Join the rows; press the seam allowances in one direction.

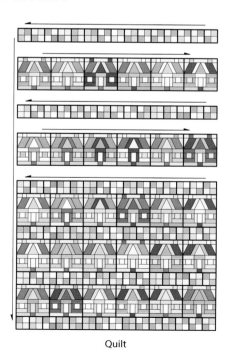

Quilt

Finishing the Quilt

For more details on quilting and finishing, go to ShopMartingale.com/HowtoQuilt.

1 Layer the backing, batting, and quilt top; baste the layers together. Hand or machine quilt as desired. The featured quilt is machine quilted with an allover flower design.

2 Use the multicolored 2½"-wide strips to make and attach the binding.

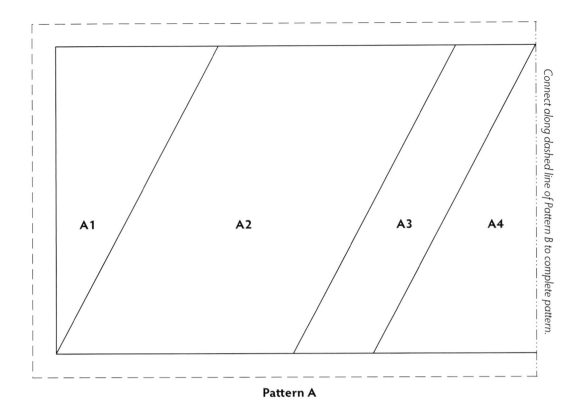

A1 A2 A3 A4

Connect along dashed line of Pattern B to complete pattern.

Pattern A

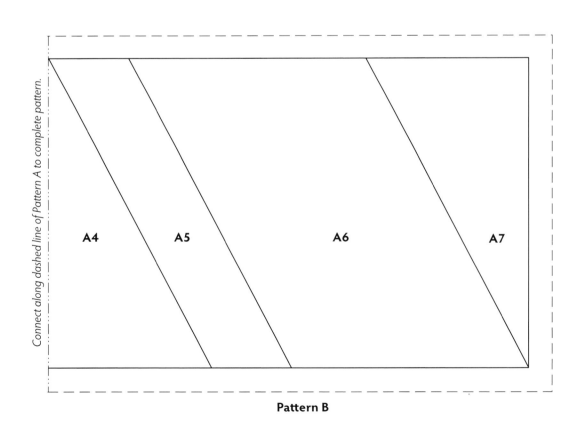

Connect along dashed line of Pattern A to complete pattern.

A4 A5 A6 A7

Pattern B

Designed and quilted by Edyta Sitar

Hay Bale

Blend a spectrum of light and dark fat eighths in classic florals, plaids, and stripes in this simple scrappy quilt.

Finished quilt: 66½" x 66½"
Finished block: 6" x 6"

Materials

Yardage is based on 42"-wide fabric unless otherwise specified. Fat eighths measure 9" x 21".

21 fat eighths of assorted light prints for blocks

21 fat eighths of assorted dark prints for blocks

1⅓ yards of stripe for border

⅝ yard of dark print for binding

4½ yards of backing fabric.

75" x 75" piece of batting

Cutting

All measurements include ¼"-wide seam allowances. From each fat eighth, you'll cut enough pieces for two blocks. Follow the cutting plan diagram below to make the best use of your fabric and be sure you have the correct sets of matching pieces needed to make the blocks.

From the assorted light prints, cut:

41 squares, 4½" x 4½" (A)

80 rectangles, 1½" x 4½" (B)

80 rectangles, 1½" x 6½" (C)

164 squares, 2½" x 2½" (D)

From the assorted dark prints, cut:

40 squares, 4½" x 4½" (A)

82 rectangles, 1½" x 4½" (B)

82 rectangles, 1½" x 6½" (C)

160 squares 2½" x 2½" (D)

From the stripe, cut:

7 strips, 6½" x 42"

From the dark print for binding, cut:

7 strips, 2½" x 42"

Cutting plan

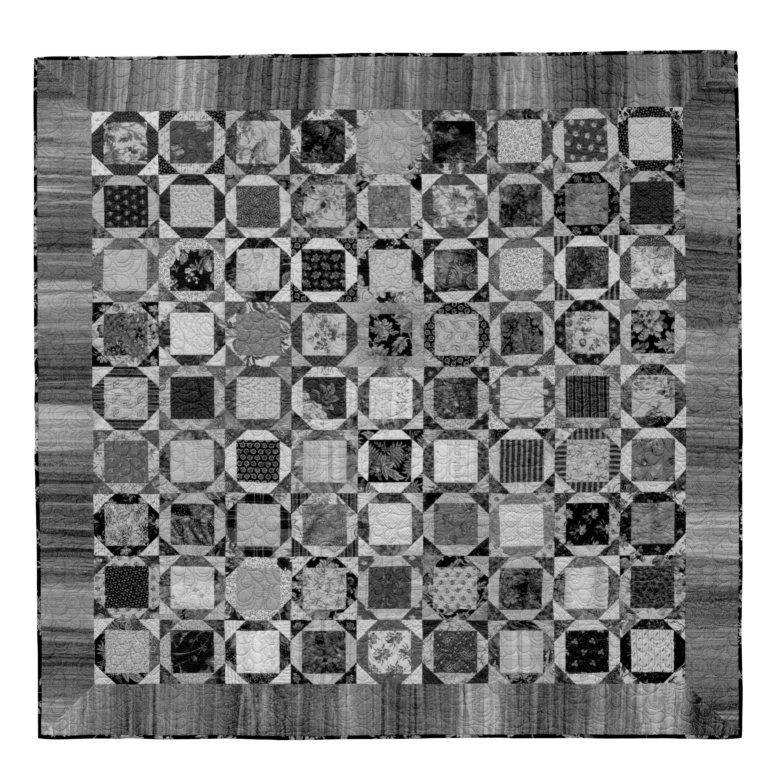

SCRAPS OF
Wisdom
FROM EDYTA SITAR

Edyta is a registered Fabricology Scrapnician whose mission is to prevent fabric stash buildup by encouraging others to utilize oodles of scraps in their quilts. Visit LaundryBasketQuilts.com.

- **A scrap that was** part of a quilt is worth saving.

- **In my dreams, the ideal scrappy quilt has at least** 1000 pieces.

- **Let me tell you a little something about how I store my scraps.** I keep them in a bushel basket.

- **When I start pulling fabrics for a scrappy quilt,** I use my rule of five: big print, medium print, small print, stripe, and polka dot. These five always make a great combination.

- **If you look at my assortment of scraps, you'll see** blue is the most prominent color. **The color you'll find the least of in my scraps is** purple.

- **The best advice I've received on choosing colors/ prints for scrap quilts was** from Grandma Anna: Don't try to match your scraps!

- **If I had a signature move, I'd say you'll know a quilt is mine by looking because** I mix print and batik scraps in my quilts.

- **Thumbs up or thumbs down? Scrappy binding?** Thumbs up. **Scrappy backing?** Thumbs down.

- **Here's my secret to keeping your ¼" seam allowances spot on:** Sit up straight exactly in line with the needle of your machine. We're sewing, not doing yoga!

Assembling the Blocks

The quilt consists of 81 blocks. Each block contains one A square, two B rectangles, two C rectangles that match the B rectangles, and four matching D squares. Forty blocks have a dark A square, light B and C rectangles, and dark D squares. Forty-one blocks have a light A square, dark B and C rectangles, and light D squares. After cutting, sort the pieces for each block before sewing.

1 Using the chosen pieces for your block, sew the light B rectangles to the top and bottom of the dark A square; press the seam allowances toward the rectangles. Sew the light C rectangles to the sides of the unit; press. The unit should measure 6½" square, including the seam allowances.

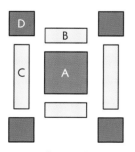

Sort for 40 blocks.

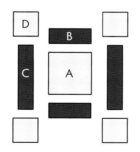

Sort for 41 blocks.

I spill my scraps all over the floor when it's time to play.

2 Draw a diagonal line from corner to corner on the wrong side of the four D squares. Place a marked D square on each corner of the pieced unit with right sides together as shown. Sew on each drawn line, and then trim the seam allowances to ¼" wide. Press the squares away from the center. The block should measure 6½" square. Repeat to make a total of 40 blocks with dark A squares.

Make 40.

3 In the same manner, assemble 41 blocks with light A squares, dark B and C rectangles, and light D squares.

Make 41.

Assembling the Quilt Top

1 Lay out nine rows of nine blocks, beginning with a light center block and alternating light and dark, as shown in the quilt assembly diagram on page 41. Join the blocks to assemble each row; press the seam allowances in alternating directions from row to row.

2 Join the rows; press the seam allowances in one direction. The quilt top should measure 54½" square, including seam allowances.

3 Join all of the stripe strips end to end; press the seam allowances in one direction. From the long strip, cut four strips, 6½" x 71". Fold each strip in half widthwise to find the center; pin-mark. Fold the quilt to find the center of each edge; pin-mark. Pin the borders to the quilt edges with right sides together, matching the centers. Stitch to the quilt top, beginning and ending ¼" from the quilt-top edges. Repeat with the remaining border strips.

4 Lay the first corner to be mitered on an ironing board. Fold under one border strip at a 45° angle to the other strip. Press and pin. Fold the quilt with right sides together, aligning the adjacent edges of the border. Stitch on the pressed crease, sewing from the previous stitching line to the outer edges. Press the seam allowances open, check the right side to make sure the miters are neat, and then trim away the excess strips, leaving ¼" seam allowance. Repeat to miter the remaining corners.

Finishing the Quilt

For more details on quilting and finishing, go to ShopMartingale.com/HowtoQuilt.

1 Layer the backing, batting, and quilt top; baste the layers together. Hand or machine quilt as desired. The featured quilt has an allover design of curving loops and feathers.

2 Use the dark-print 2½"-wide strips to make and attach the binding.

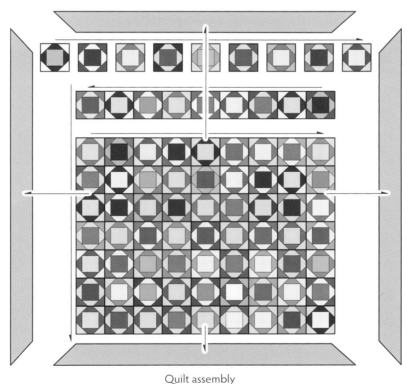

Quilt assembly

This simple Nine Patch quilt is reminiscent of a colorful collection of buttons. Mix and match an eclectic array of bright prints for the scrappy blocks.

Finished quilt: 59½" x 75½"
Finished block: 6" x 6"

Designed by Sherri McConnell; quilted by Maggi Honeyman

Button Box

Materials

Yardage is based on 42"-wide fabric unless otherwise specified. Fat quarters measure 18" x 21".

32 squares *each*, 2½" x 2½", of assorted red, pink, and yellow prints for Button blocks (96 total)*

40 squares *each*, 2½" x 2½", of assorted blue and green prints for Button blocks (80 total)*

48 squares, 2½" x 2½", of assorted aqua prints for Button blocks*

24 squares, 2½" x 2½", of assorted orange prints for Button blocks*

1⅛ yards of aqua dot print for contrast blocks and cornerstones

7 fat quarters of assorted light prints for Button blocks and sashing**

⅔ yard of white solid for contrast blocks

¾ yard of text print for border

⅝ yard of blue print for binding

3¾ yards of backing fabric

68" x 84" piece of batting

For a very scrappy look, use an assortment of precut 2½" mini charm squares and/or scraps from leftover Jelly Roll strips and 5" charm squares.

**Use more than 7 fat quarters for a scrappier look.*

Cutting

All measurements include ¼"-wide seam allowances.

From the aqua dot, cut:

13 strips, 2½" x 42", crosscut 3 of the strips into 48 squares, 2½" x 2½"

1 strip, 3" x 42", crosscut into 4 squares, 3" x 3"

From the assorted light prints, cut:

42 strips, 2½" x 21"; crosscut into:
  110 rectangles, 2½" x 6½"
  31 squares, 2½" x 2½"

From the white solid, cut:

8 strips, 2½" x 42"

Continued on page 44

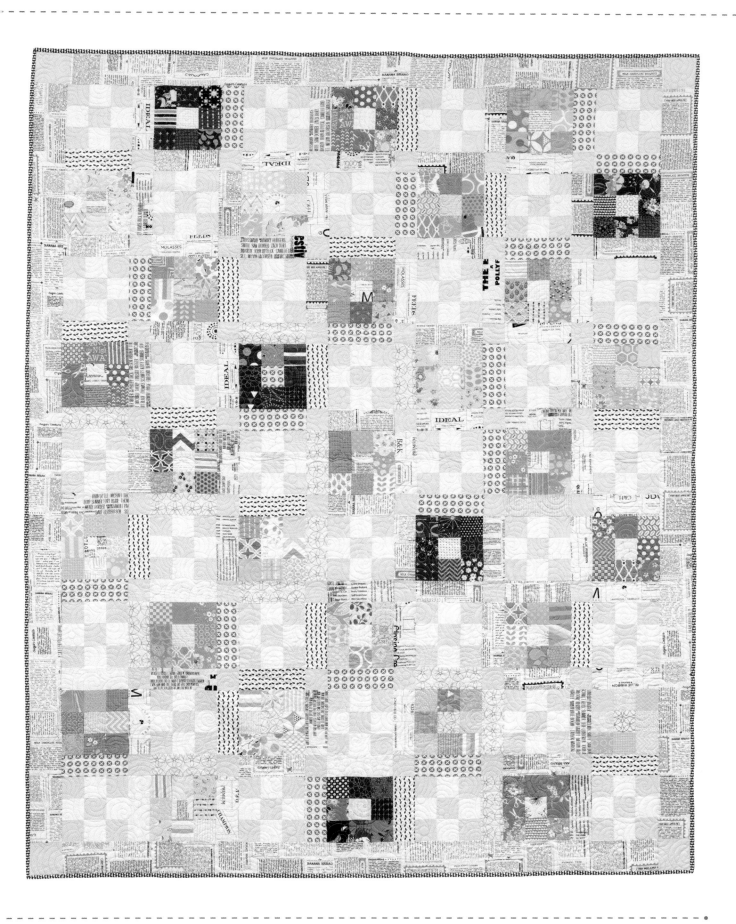

Continued from page 42

From the text print, cut:
7 strips, 3" x 42"*

From the blue print, cut:
7 strips, 2½" x 42"

Wait to cut the text-print border pieces until the quilt center is complete and you've checked the measurements.

" *One tip that will make creating my quilt more accurate is this: Make sure the Nine Patch blocks are accurate. It's all easy when they measure just right!* "

Assembling the Blocks

The quilt contains 31 Button blocks and 32 Nine Patch blocks.

1 Group the bright 2½" squares by color. Select eight assorted bright squares and one light 2½" square for each block. Sew two rows of three bright squares; press the seam allowances toward the center. Sew two bright squares to opposite sides of one light square to make the center row of the block. Press the seam allowances away from the center.

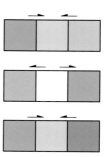

SCRAPS OF
Wisdom
FROM SHERRI McCONNELL

Sherri is a scrap-happy sewist whose scraptacular quilt creations reflect her enthusiasm for fabrics aplenty. Visit AQuiltingLife.com.

- **A scrap that is** 1½" square is not too small to save.

- **In my dreams, the ideal scrappy quilt has at least** 100 different fabrics in it!

- **Let me tell you a little something about how I store my scraps.** I sort by color and by type—squares of all sizes and strips of varying widths.

- **When I start pulling fabrics for a scrappy quilt,** I begin by picking a color scheme and then pull a few fabrics from each color to get started.

- **If you look at my assortment of scraps, you'll see** blue is the most prominent color. **The color you'll find the least of in my scraps is** purple.

- **The best advice I've received on choosing colors/ prints for scrap quilts was** to take a photograph on my phone and look at the mix in the photo.

- **If I had a signature move, I'd say you'll know a quilt is mine by looking because** it has a red binding, my most commonly used binding color.

- **Thumbs up or thumbs down? Scrappy binding?** Thumbs up. **Scrappy backing?** Thumbs up.

- **Here's my secret to keeping your ¼" seam allowances spot on:** I use a ¼" foot but also have to move my needle a little to the right before sewing.

2 Sew the bright rows to the top and bottom of the center row. Press the seam allowances away from the center. Make 31 Button blocks.

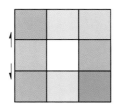

Make 31 blocks, 6½" square.

3 Sew a white strip between two aqua strips. Make four strip sets. Press the seam allowances away from the center. Crosscut the strip sets into 64 segments, 2½" wide.

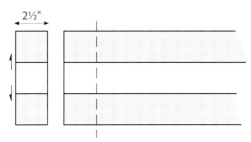

Make 4 strip sets.
Cut 64 segments.

4 Sew one aqua strip between two white strips. Make two strip sets. Press the seam allowances toward the aqua strips. Crosscut the strip sets into 32 center segments, 2½" wide.

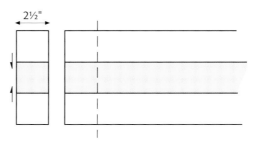

Make 2 strip sets.
Cut 32 segments.

5 Join two segments from step 3 to a segment from step 4. Press the seam allowances toward the top and bottom. Make 32 Nine Patch blocks.

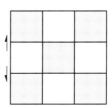

Make 32 blocks, 6½" square.

Assembling the Quilt Top

1 Lay out the blocks in nine rows of seven blocks each as shown below, alternating the Nine Patch and Button blocks. Place six light 2½" x 6½" sashing rectangles between the blocks in each row as shown. Join into rows. Press the seam allowances toward the sashing strips.

2 Lay out eight sashing rows consisting of seven light 2½" x 6½" rectangles and six aqua 2½" squares in each row. Begin and end each sashing row with a rectangle as shown. Join the rectangles and squares in each sashing row. Press the seam allowances toward the rectangles.

3 Join the block and sashing rows; press the seam allowances in one direction.

4 Join the text-print 3" x 42" strips end to end. From the joined strips, cut two side borders, 3" x 70½", and two top and bottom borders, 3" x 54½". Sew the aqua 3" squares to both ends of the top and bottom borders. Sew the side borders to the sides of the quilt; press the seam allowances toward the borders. Sew the top and bottom borders to the top and bottom of the quilt; press.

Finishing the Quilt

For more details on quilting and finishing, go to ShopMartingale.com/HowtoQuilt.

1 Layer the backing, batting, and quilt top; baste the layers together. Hand or machine quilt as desired. The featured quilt has an allover design of circles and spirals.

2 Use the blue-print 2½"-wide strips to make and attach the binding.

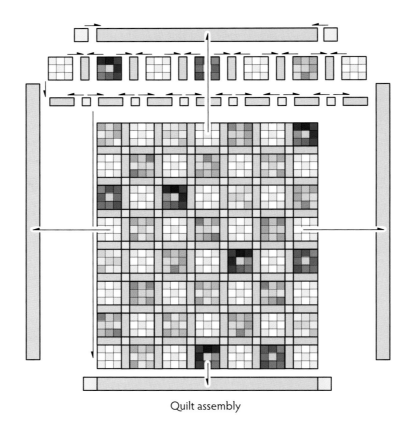

Quilt assembly

Sew cozy flannel scraps into a striking diamond design using a simple half-square-triangle pattern.

Finished quilt: 60½" x 75½"
Finished block: 7½" x 7½"

Designed and quilted by Lisa Bongean

Flight Path

Materials

Yardage is based on 42"-wide fabric unless otherwise specified. Flannel fat eighths measure 9" x 21"; check prior to cutting to ensure the pieces are at least 21" wide.

40 Wool & Needle flannel fat eighths of assorted dark prints for blocks

25 flannel fat eighths of assorted light prints for blocks

½ yard of dark houndstooth flannel for binding

4 yards of flannel for backing

67" x 82" piece of batting

Primitive Gatherings 1½" Finished Triangle Paper (optional)

Cutting

All measurements include scant ¼"-wide seam allowances.

From the assorted dark prints, cut:
40 squares, 8⅜" x 8⅜"; cut in half diagonally to yield 2 triangles (80 total)
400 squares, 2⅜" x 2⅜"

From the assorted light prints, cut:
600 squares, 2⅜" x 2⅜"; cut *200 of the squares* in half diagonally to yield 2 triangles (400 total)

From the dark houndstooth, cut:
7 strips, 2⅛" x 42"*

*Flannel is bulkier than quilting cotton, so Lisa used 2⅛"-wide binding strips for a narrow binding.

" *To help create this quilt more easily and accurately, I recommend using 1½"-finished half-square triangle papers from Primitive Gatherings.* "

Assembling the Half-Square-Triangle Units

The quilt is composed of 80 blocks. Each block requires one large dark triangle, 10 light/dark half-square-triangle units, and five light triangles. If desired, use triangle-piecing papers to make the half-square-triangle units, or use the following method.

1 Draw a diagonal line from corner to corner on the light squares. Place one light and one dark 2⅜" square right sides together with the light square on top. Stitch ¼" from both sides of the drawn line.

2 Cut the squares along the drawn lines to yield two half-square-triangle units. Press the seam allowances toward the dark prints. The units should be 2" square, including seam allowances. Repeat to make 800 half-square-triangle units.

Make 800.

Assembling the Blocks

1 Lay out 10 half-square-triangle units and five light triangles in five rows as shown. Join the units and triangles in each row, pressing the seam allowances in alternating directions. Join the rows; press the seam allowances in one direction. Make 80 pieced triangles.

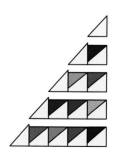 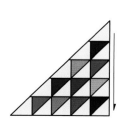

Piecing with Paper

When a quilt calls for many small half-square-triangle units, triangle piecing paper, such as Primitive Gatherings 1½" Finished Triangle Paper, will save you time and stress. The paper allows you to accurately sew and cut several units at once. Layer a sheet of the paper over two fabrics placed right sides together, and then stitch along the lines according to the manufacturer's instructions. Cut the stitched fabric, remove the paper, and then press the seam allowances as directed to reveal a perfectly stitched half-square-triangle unit.

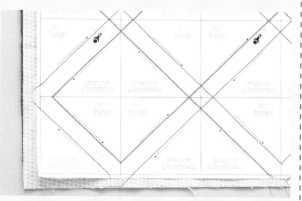

Stitch along the printed lines as indicated.

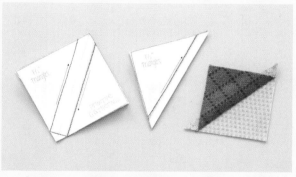

Cut apart and press the half-square triangle units.

2 Place a dark triangle and pieced triangle right
sides together. Sew the long diagonal edge.
Press the seam allowances toward the dark triangle
and trim the dog-ears. Make 80 blocks that are 8"
square, including the seam allowances.

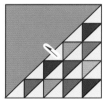

Make 80.

Assembling the Quilt Top

1 Lay out the blocks in eight rows of 10, rotating
the blocks as shown opposite to create the
diamond Barn Raising setting.

2 Join the blocks in each row. Press the seam
allowances in alternating directions from row
to row. Join the rows; press the seam allowances in
one direction.

Finishing the Quilt

For more details on quilting and finishing, go to
ShopMartingale.com/HowtoQuilt.

1 Layer the backing, batting, and quilt top; baste
the layers together. Hand or machine quilt as
desired. The featured quilt was machine quilted
with an allover swirl design.

2 Use the dark houndstooth 2⅛"-wide strips to
make and attach the binding.

SCRAPS OF
Wisdom
FROM LISA BONGEAN

Lisa is the maven of miniature in a small, small world where teeny-tiny scraps come together to make spectacular scrappy quilts. Visit LisaBongean.com.

- **A scrap that is** 1" square is not too small to save.

- **In my dreams, the ideal scrappy quilt has at least** 250 different fabrics in it!

- **Let me tell you a little something about how I sort my scraps.** I sort in strips or squares of 3½" or less, all the way to 1".

- **When I start pulling fabrics for a scrappy quilt,** I begin by figuring out the best use of fabric, especially 5" charms, 10" squares, or fat eighths.

- **If you look at my assortment of scraps, you'll see** tans/backgrounds are the most prominent colors. **The color you'll find the least of in my scraps is** white.

- **The best advice I've received on choosing colors/ prints for scrap quilts was** the more the merrier.

- **If I had a signature move, I'd say you'll know a quilt is mine by looking because** it was made with a bunch of tiny triangles.

- **Thumbs up or thumbs down? Scrappy binding?** Thumbs down. **Scrappy backing?** Thumbs up.

- **Here's my secret to keeping your ¼" seam allowance spot on:** Use pretty duct tape as a guide.

Quilt assembly

Designed by Corey Yoder; quilted by Abby Latimer

Meadow

Mix a cheerful assortment of precut strips to make this simple block that forms a pretty chain-like pattern.

Finished quilt: 88" x 107"
Finished block: 9" x 9"

Materials

Yardage is based on 42"-wide fabric.

80 assorted print strips, 2½" x 42", for blocks

5½ yards of white solid for background

1⅓ yards of floral print for outer border

½ yard of light-green print for inner border

1 yard of gray gingham for binding

8 yards of backing fabric

93" x 112" piece of batting

Cutting

All measurements include ¼"-wide seam allowances.

From *each* assorted strip, cut:
8 rectangles, 2½" x 5" (640 total)

From the white solid, cut:
40 strips, 2½" x 42"; crosscut into 640 squares, 2½" x 2½"
93 strips, 1" x 42"; crosscut *58 of the strips* into:
    320 strips, 1" x 5"
    70 strips, 1" x 9½"

From the light-green print, cut:
9 strips, 1½" x 42"

From the floral print, cut:
10 strips, 4½" x 42"

From the gray gingham, cut:
10 strips, 2½" x 42"

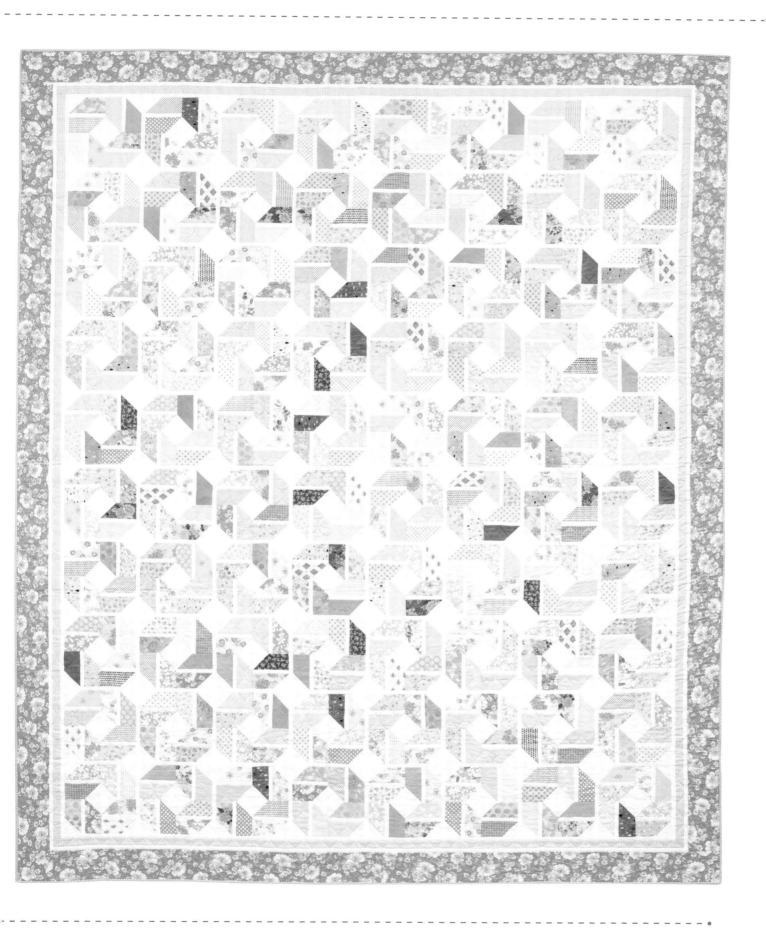

SCRAPS OF
Wisdom
FROM COREY YODER

Corey is Captain Scraptastic when it comes to perfecting the art of scrappy quilts. Follow this leader by visiting LittleMissShabby.com.

- **A scrap that is** 1" square is not too small to save.

- **In my dreams, the ideal scrappy quilt has at least** 500 different fabrics in it!

- **Let me tell you a little something about how I store my scraps.** I have an ongoing, overflowing scrap bin that periodically gets sorted into smaller bins by color, or picked through to find all of the good bits that have settled to the bottom.

- **When I start pulling fabrics for a scrappy quilt,** I begin by settling on a color story and choosing fabrics accordingly.

- **If you look at my assortment of scraps, you'll see a** rainbow of colors. **The color you'll find the least of in my scraps is** purple.

- **The best advice I've received on choosing colors/ prints for scrap quilts was** to pay attention to scale. Scrap quilts often utilize many smaller pieces and those large-scale fabrics won't play as nicely.

- **If I had a signature move, I'd say you'll know a quilt is mine by looking because** it uses scrappy brights and lots of white.

- **Thumbs up or thumbs down? Scrappy binding?** Way up. **Scrappy backing?** Definitely.

- **Here's my secret to keeping your ¼" seam allowances spot on:** Accuracy in each step from cutting to sewing to pressing.

Assembling the Blocks

1 Sew a white 1" x 5" strip between two different print 2½" x 5" rectangles as shown. Make 320 pieced units measuring 5" square, including the seam allowances.

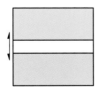

Make 320.

2 Draw a diagonal line from corner to corner on the wrong side of each white square. Place two white squares on opposite corners of each pieced unit, right sides together as shown. Sew along the marked lines, and then trim the seam allowances to ¼". Press the squares open.

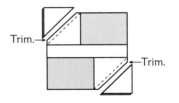

Trim. —Trim.

3 Arrange four pieced units in two rows of two, rotating them as shown. Join the units in each row; press the seam allowances in opposite directions. Join the rows; press the seam allowances in one direction. Make 80 blocks measuring 9½" square, including seam allowances.

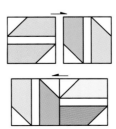
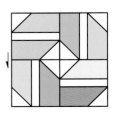

Make 80.

Assembling the Quilt Top

1 Lay out the blocks in 10 rows of eight blocks each with a white 1" x 9½" strip between blocks as shown. Join the blocks and strips in each row. Press the seam allowances toward the strips.

2 Join 17 of the white 1" x 42" strips end to end, and then crosscut the long strip into nine strips, 1" x 76". Place the strips between the rows. Join the rows and strips; press the seam allowances toward the strips.

3 Join the remaining 18 white 1" x 42" strips end to end, and then crosscut the long strip into two strips, 1" x 95"; two strips, 1" x 77"; two strips, 1" x 98"; and two strips, 1" x 80". Sew the 1" x 95" strips to the sides of the quilt top; press the seam allowances toward the strips. Sew the 1" x 77" strips to the top and bottom of the quilt top; press.

4 Join the green 1½" x 42" strips end to end, and then crosscut the long strip into two strips, 1½" x 96", and two strips, 1½" x 79". Sew the strips to the quilt top in the same manner as step 3. Repeat to add the white 1" x 98" strips and 1" x 80" strips to the quilt top.

5 Join the floral strips end to end, and then crosscut the long strip into two strips, 4½" x 99", and two strips, 4½" x 88". Sew the strips to the quilt top in the same manner as the previous borders.

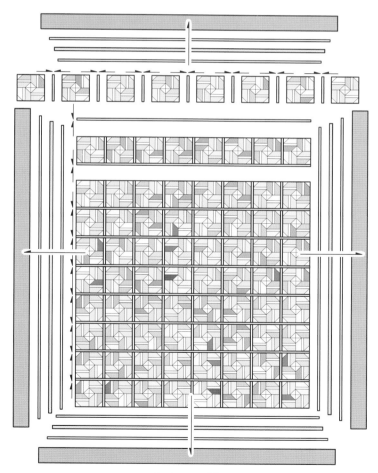

Quilt assembly

Finishing the Quilt

For more details on quilting and finishing, go to ShopMartingale.com/HowtoQuilt.

1 Layer the backing, batting, and quilt top; baste the layers together. Hand or machine quilt as desired. The featured quilt was machine quilted with parallel wavy lines that complement the chain-like pattern of the blocks.

2 Use the gray-gingham 2½"-wide strips to make and attach the binding.

Sew with a friend. Nothing beats an afternoon of sewing and gabbing. You'll be amazed how quickly the time passes.

Designed by Jan Ragaller; quilted by Kelly Edwards

Summer in the City

Bright and bold batiks sparkle in this design that combines scrappy Rail Fence and Hourglass blocks. Setting the blocks on point adds a sense of fun and movement.

Finished quilt: 64⅛" x 74¾"
Finished block: 7½" x 7½"

Materials

Yardage is based on 42"-wide fabric unless otherwise specified.
Fat quarters measure 18" x 21". Fat eighths measure 9" x 21".

53 assorted bright batik strips, 2½" x 42", for blocks*

22 assorted bright batik fat eighths *OR* 11 bright batik fat quarters for blocks*

⅝ yard of lime batik for binding

4 yards of backing fabric

71" x 81" piece of batting

*This is the minimum quantity needed. Choose more strips and fat eighths for more variety.

Cutting

All measurements include ¼"-wide seam allowances.
From *each* batik strip, cut:
2 lengthwise strips, 1¼" x 42" (106 total); crosscut in half to yield 212 total strips, 1¼" x 21" (2 are extra)
From the batik fat eighths or fat quarters, cut a *total* of:
42 squares, 8¾" x 8¾"
2 squares, 6¼" x 6¼" (cut from different prints)
From the lime batik, cut:
7 strips, 2¼" x 42"

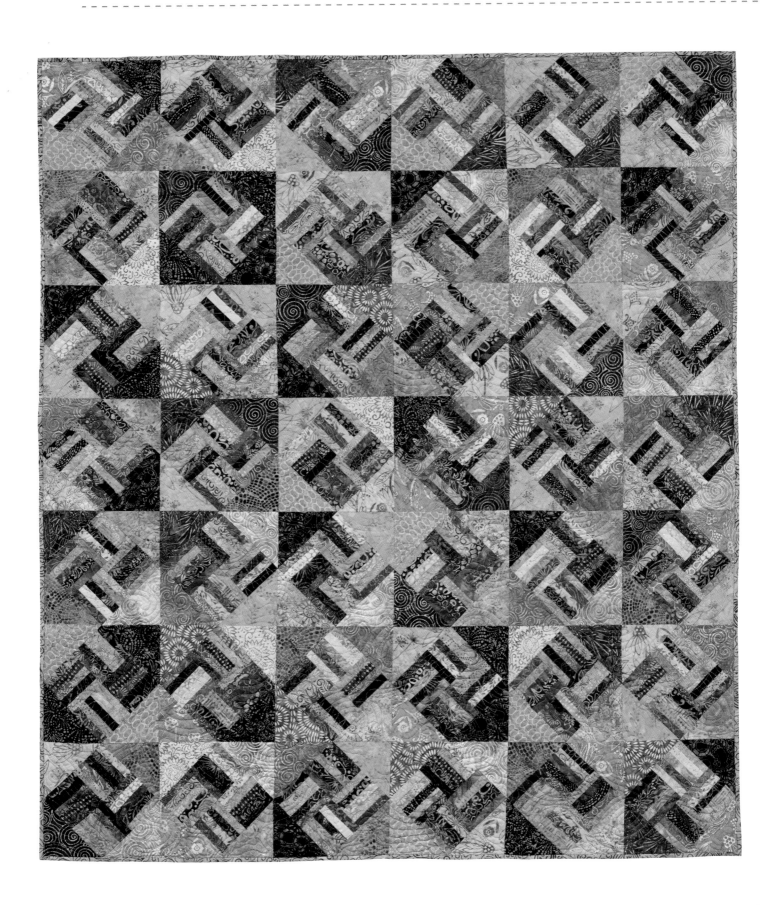

Jan is a PhD in Scrap Quilt Mania and by PhD we mean, Piled High and Deep in her quest to collect the most scraps. She is both one of us and the best of us!

- **A scrap that is** 2" x 4" is not too small for me to save.

- **In my dreams, the ideal scrappy quilt has at least** 100 different fabrics in it. I don't know, can you really have too many?!

- **Let me tell you a little something about how I sort my scraps.** I have baskets, tubs, and bins full of fabric and scraps. I try to keep them color coordinated, but in my enthusiasm for planning my next project, that organization is the first to fail!

- **When I start pulling fabrics for a scrappy quilt,** I begin with the overall style of the quilt—contemporary, modern, shabby chic, or whatever style I'm feeling like. Then I pick the main print and go from there.

- **If you look at my assortment of scraps, you'll see** red, green, and purple are the most prominent colors. **The color you'll find the least of in my scraps is** yellow or brown.

- **If I had a signature move, I'd say you'll know a quilt is mine by looking because** it usually has a pieced border or two.

- **Thumbs up or thumbs down? Scrappy binding?** No thank you. **Scrappy backing?** Sure! I do that quite often.

- **Here's my secret to keeping your ¼" seam allowance spot on:** Use a ¼" presser foot and double-check it for accuracy.

Assembling the Rail Fence Blocks

1 Sew five batik strips along the long edges in a scrappy fashion to make a 4¼" x 21" strip set. Press the seam allowances in one direction. Make 42 strip sets. Cut each strip set into four segments, 4¼" wide, for a total of 168 segments.

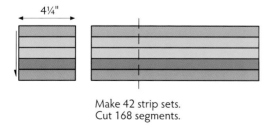

4¼"

Make 42 strip sets.
Cut 168 segments.

2 Lay out four segments in two rows as shown. Join the segments in each row; press the seam allowances in alternate directions. Join the rows to complete the 8" square block, which includes seam allowances. Make 42 Rail Fence blocks.

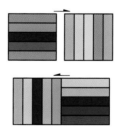

Make 42 blocks,
8" square.

" The best advice I've received on mixing colors and fabrics for scrap quilts is that they'll all go together—if you put it in, it goes! "

Assembling the Hourglass Blocks

1 Draw a diagonal line from corner to corner on the wrong side of 21 of the 8¾" squares. Place a marked and unmarked square with right sides together. Sew ¼" from both sides of the drawn line. Cut along the drawn line to yield two half-square-triangle units. Press the seam allowances in one direction. Make 42 half-square-triangle units. Reserve 12 units to use for the setting triangles.

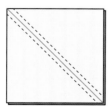 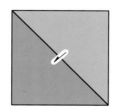

Make 42.

2 Group 30 of the half-square-triangle units in 15 pairs, mixing the colors in a scrappy fashion. Place one pair with right sides together, aligning and interlocking the seams. Draw a diagonal line on the wrong side of one unit from corner to corner, perpendicular to the seam. Sew ¼" from both sides of the drawn line. Cut along the drawn line to yield two Hourglass blocks measuring 8" square. Press the seam allowances in one direction. Make 30 Hourglass blocks.

Make 30 blocks, 8" square.

Making the Setting Triangles

1 Cut the 12 reserved half-square triangles in half diagonally, perpendicular to the seam, to yield 24 pieced setting triangles (two are extra).

Make 24.

2 Cut the two batik 6¼" squares in half diagonally to yield four corner triangles.

Assembling the Quilt Top

Lay out the Rail Fence blocks, Hourglass blocks, and setting triangles in 12 diagonal rows as shown in the quilt assembly diagram. Place the corner triangles in the corners. Join the pieces in each row; press the seam allowances toward the Hourglass blocks and setting triangles. Join the rows; press the seam allowances in one direction. Add the corner triangles last. Press.

Finishing the Quilt

For more details on quilting and finishing, go to ShopMartingale.com/HowtoQuilt.

1 Layer the backing, batting, and quilt top; baste the layers together. Hand or machine quilt as desired. The featured quilt was machine quilted with an allover swirl and spiral design.

2 Use the lime 2¼"-wide strips to make and attach the binding.

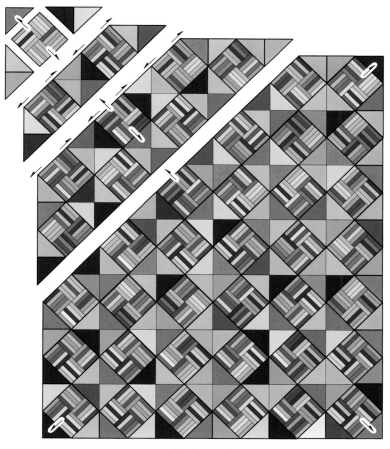

Quilt assembly

A combination of charming floral, gingham, and dot prints gives this scrappy quilt a sweet vintage feel. The large blocks are a unique combination of a flower and cross design.

Finished quilt: 75¾" x 90½"
Finished block: 12¾" x 12¾"

Designed by Susan Ache; quilted by Valerie Sneed

In Bloom

Materials

*Yardage is based on 42"-wide fabric unless otherwise specified.
Fat quarters measure 18" x 21".*

30 assorted medium-print fat quarters for blocks and cornerstones

30 assorted light-print fat quarters for background and sashing

¾ yard of floral print for binding

5½ yards of backing fabric

82" x 97" piece of batting

Cutting

All measurements include scant ¼"-wide seam allowances.

From *each* of the 30 medium fat quarters, cut:

5 strips, 2" x 21"; crosscut into:
    4 rectangles, 2" x 3" (120 total)
    8 rectangles, 2" x 4½" (240 total)
    4 rectangles, 2" x 6" (120 total)

2 strips, 2¼" x 21", crosscut into:
    4 rectangles, 2¼" x 6" (120 total)
    1 square, 2¼" x 2¼" (30 total)

1 strip, 1½" x 10" (30 total; 2 are extra)

From *each* of 30 light fat quarters, cut:*

2 or 3 lengthwise strips, 2½" x 13¼" (71 total)

1 lengthwise strip, 3½" x 8"; crosscut into 4 squares, 3½" x 3½"
    (120 total)

1 lengthwise strip, 3" x 18"; crosscut into 4 squares, 3" x 3"
    (120 total)

2 lengthwise strips, 2" x 18"; crosscut into 16 squares, 2" x 2"
    (480 total)

From the floral print, cut:

9 strips, 2½" x 42"

*Lengthwise strips are cut parallel to the selvage edge, or along the 18" length of the fat quarter.

Susan is a scrap mason building incredible scrappy quilts block by block. She's also never without one more idea up her sleeve for artfully using those scraps!

- **A scrap that is** 2" square is not too small for me to save. All my leftover cuttings from triangle piecing also get saved.

- **In my dreams, the ideal scrappy quilt has over** 100 different fabrics in it!

- **Let me tell you a little something about how I sort my scraps.** I sort strips by size in drawers. Squares are stored in containers. And all triangle cuttings are stacked in boxes.

- **When I start pulling fabrics for a scrappy quilt,** I begin by making one block to see what color range I want to play with. Then it is a matter of pulling anything and everything that works with that block.

- **If you look at my assortment of scraps, you'll see** anything in a shade of blue is the most prominent color. **The color you'll find the least of in my scraps is** purple. I don't think I even own one piece of purple in my entire stash!

- **If I had a signature move, I'd say you'll know a quilt is mine by looking because** it always has tons of different blocks.

- **Thumbs up or thumbs down? Scrappy binding?** No. **Scrappy backing?** Only when I want something in a hurry and there isn't enough of my favorite fabric.

- **Here's my secret to keeping your ¼" seam allowances spot on:** I pay attention to the one perfect mark on my machine, and it never fails.

Assembling the Blocks

Each block requires two medium prints and one light print. Plan and group the pieces for each block before you begin sewing in order to create fabric combinations that you like.

1 Select two medium prints for the cross and flower sections of each block. From the first print (center square and petals), select a matching set of the following pieces: four rectangles, 2" x 3"; four rectangles, 2" x 4½"; and one square, 2¼". From the second print (cross bars and diagonal strips), select a matching set of the following pieces: four rectangles, 2" x 4½"; four rectangles, 2" x 6"; and four rectangles, 2¼" x 6".

2 From the light prints, for each block select a matching set of 16 squares, 2"; four squares, 3"; and four squares, 3½". Draw a diagonal line from corner to corner on the wrong side of the 2" and 3½" squares.

3 Place a marked light 2" square on one end of a medium 2" x 3" rectangle with right sides together as shown. Sew on the marked line. Trim the seam allowances to ¼". Press the square away from the rectangle and press open the seam allowances. Make four. Repeat to sew a marked light 2" square to the end of a medium 2" x 4½" rectangle in the same manner. Make four.

Make 4.

Make 4.

4 Sew a shorter pieced unit from step 3 to one side of a light 3" square as shown. Press the seam allowances toward the square. Sew a longer pieced unit to the bottom as shown; press. Make four units that are 4½" square.

Make 4.

One tip that will make piecing my quilt more accurate is to pay attention to the direction you press the seam allowances and make sure they're exactly ¼".

5 Place a marked light 2" square right sides together with a medium 2" x 4½" rectangle as shown. Sew on the marked line. Trim the seam allowances to ¼". Press the square away from the rectangle, and then press open the seam allowances. Make four. Repeat to sew a marked light 2" square to a medium 2" x 6" rectangle in the same manner. Make four.

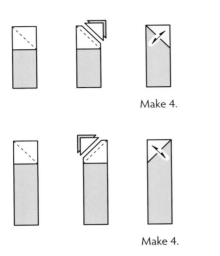

Make 4.

Make 4.

6 Sew the units from step 5 to the units from step 4 as shown. Make four units that are 6" square, including seam allowances.

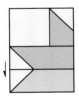
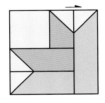

Make 4.

7 Place a marked light 3½" square on the lower-right corner of a pieced unit with right sides together as shown. Sew on the marked line. Trim the seam allowances to ¼", and then press the square away from the pieced unit. Make four flower units that are 6" square.

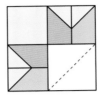
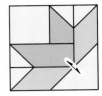

Make 4.

8 Arrange the four flower units, the medium 2¼" square, and the four medium 2¼" x 6" rectangles in three rows as shown. Join the pieces in each row; press the seam allowances in alternating directions from row to row. Join the rows; press the seam allowances toward the center row. Make 30 Flower blocks that are 13¼" square, including seam allowances.

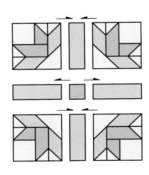
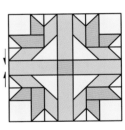

Make 30.

Assembling the Quilt Top

1 Join two medium 1½" x 10" strips. Press the seam allowance toward the darker print. Make 14 strips sets. Crosscut each strip set into six segments, 1½" wide, for a total of 84 segments.

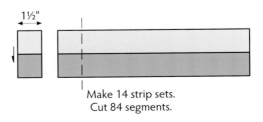

Make 14 strip sets.
Cut 84 segments.

2 Join the segments in scrappy pairs to make 42 four-patch cornerstones.

Make 42.

3 Join five light 2½" x 13¼" strips and six four-patch cornerstones as shown to make a sashing row. Make seven sashing rows. Lay out six rows of five blocks and six light 2½" x 13¼" strips as shown. Join the blocks and strips in each row. Lay out the block and sashing rows as shown. Join the rows; press the seam allowances toward the sashing.

Finishing the Quilt

For more details on quilting and finishing, go to ShopMartingale.com/HowtoQuilt.

1 Layer the backing, batting, and quilt top; baste the layers together. Hand or machine quilt as desired. The featured quilt was machine quilted with an allover leaf and feather design.

2 Use the floral 2½"-wide strips to make and attach the binding.

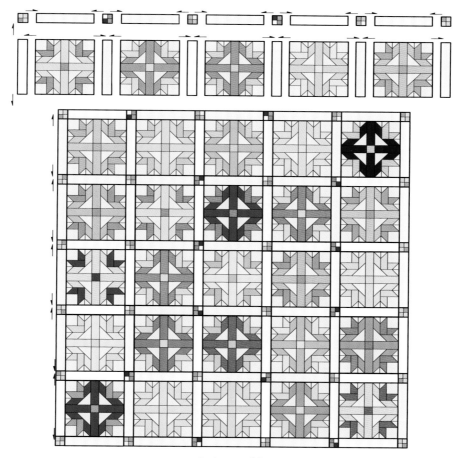

Quilt assembly

Missouri Roads

A simple scrappy quilt brings to mind a map of winding roads. Leftover precut 2½" strips and 5" charm squares work perfectly for the quick and easy blocks.

Finished quilt: 63½" x 79½"
Finished block: 8" x 8"

Materials

Yardage is based on 42"-wide fabric.

Approximately 4 charm packs (144 squares *total*, 5" x 5") *OR* 2½ yards *total* of assorted medium purple, tan, green, and pink prints for blocks

1 Jelly Roll *OR* 2½ yards of beige tone on tone for background and inner border

2 yards of purple floral for outer border and binding

4 yards of backing fabric

70" x 86" piece of batting

Cutting

All measurements include ¼"-wide seam allowances.

From the assorted charm squares, cut:

48 squares in quarters to yield 192 squares, 2½" x 2½"; trim the remaining 96 squares to 4½" x 4½"

From the beige tone on tone, cut:

32 strips, 2½" x 42"; crosscut 24 into 384 squares, 2½" x 2½"

From the purple floral, cut:

8 strips, 6" x 42"

8 strips, 2½" x 42"

SCRAPS OF
Wisdom
FROM JENNY DOAN

Jenny is the queen-of-quite-a-lot when it comes to having a stash of precuts to pull from. But she uses her powers for good (scrap quilts, that is) and rules with few rules other than this: Enjoy the journey. Visit MissouriStarQuiltCo.com.

- **A scrap that is** 2½" square is not too small to save.

- **In my dreams, the ideal scrappy quilt has at least** a zillion different fabrics in it. A lot!

- **Let me tell you a little something about how I sort my scraps.** I use Ziploc bags and bins. I also keep sizes like all my 2½" strips together.

- **When I start pulling fabrics for a scrappy quilt,** I begin with my favorite colors.

- **If you look at my assortment of scraps, you'll see** blue is the most prominent color. **The color you'll find the least of in my scraps is** yellow.

- **The best advice I've received on choosing colors/ prints for scrap quilts was** to find a friend who is good with color to shop with!

- **If I had a signature move, I'd say you'll know a quilt is mine by looking because** it was made of precuts, and I often take an ordinary block and cut it up!

- **Thumbs up or thumbs down? Scrappy binding?** Love it. **Scrappy backing?** Love it.

- **Here's my secret to keeping your ¼" seam allowances spot on:** I use the edge of my presser foot. I am consistent, not perfect.

Assembling the Blocks

1 Sew together one beige and one medium print 2½" square. Press the seam allowances toward the print square. Make 192 units. Then sew the units together in pairs as shown to make 96 four-patch units that are 4½" square.

2 Draw a diagonal line from corner to corner on the wrong side of the remaining beige 2½" squares. Place two marked squares on opposite corners of a medium 4½" square as shown. Sew on the marked lines. Trim the seam allowances to ¼". Press the small squares away from the large square. Make 96 units that are 4½" square.

Make 192.

Make 96.

Make 96.

3 Lay out two four-patch units and two square units in two rows as shown. Join the units in each row; press the seam allowances in alternating directions. Join the two rows to complete the block; press the seam allowances in one direction. Make 48 blocks that are 8½" square, including seam allowances.

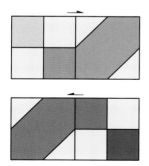
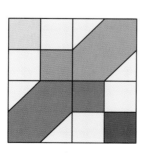

Make 48.

Assembling the Quilt Top

1 Lay out eight rows of six blocks each, rotating the blocks to create the pattern as shown in the quilt assembly diagram below. Join the blocks in each row; press the seam allowances in alternating directions from row to row. Join the rows; press the seam allowances in one direction. The quilt center should be 48½" x 64½", including seam allowances.

2 Join two beige 2½" strips end to end. Make four. Measure the width of the quilt through the center, and then trim two of the strip units to the measurement. Sew the trimmed strips to the top and bottom of the quilt. Press the seam allowances toward the strips. Measure the length of the quilt through the center. Use the remaining beige strip sets to make and attach the side borders.

3 In the same manner, join and trim the 6"-wide purple-floral strips to be the quilt's outer borders.

Finishing the Quilt

For more details on quilting and finishing, go to ShopMartingale.com/HowtoQuilt.

1 Layer the backing, batting, and quilt top; baste the layers together. Hand or machine quilt as desired. The featured quilt was machine quilted with an allover swirl design.

2 Use the purple-floral 2½"-wide strips to make and attach the binding.

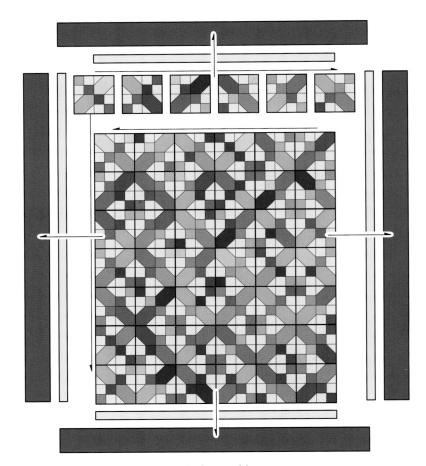

Quilt assembly

Designed by Lissa Alexander; quilted by Maggi Honeyman

My Favorite Color

Make a bold statement by showcasing a variety of scraps united by a common color family. Use a spectrum of scraps in reds, corals, and pinks like Lissa did, or choose scraps in your own favorite color for the blocks.

Finished quilt: 65" x 86"
Finished block: 8½" x 8½"

Materials

Yardage is based on 42"-wide fabric.

4 yards *total* of assorted red, pink, and coral scraps for blocks and cornerstones*

4 yards *total* of assorted light scraps for background*

2¼ yards *total* of assorted gray scraps for sashing

⅔ yard *total* of red and gray prints for binding*

6 yards of backing fabric

73" x 94" piece of batting

For a fun varied look, incorporate a Jelly Roll of assorted tones and prints to use for the 2½" x 42" strips, 2½" x 2½" squares, and binding.

Cutting

All measurements include ¼"-wide seam allowances.

From the red scraps, cut:
5 strips, 5½" x 42"
27 strips, 3" x 42"
4 strips, 2½" x 42"
9 squares, 2½" x 2½"

From the gray scraps, cut:
8 strips, 9" x 42"; crosscut *4 of the strips* into 56 rectangles, 2½" x 9"

From the light scraps, cut:
5 strips, 4" x 42"; crosscut into 96 rectangles, 2" x 4"
5 strips, 3" x 42"
10 strips, 2¼" x 42"
28 strips, 2" x 42"
8 strips, 1¾" x 42"

From the red and gray prints for binding, cut a *total* of:
8 strips, 2½" x 42"

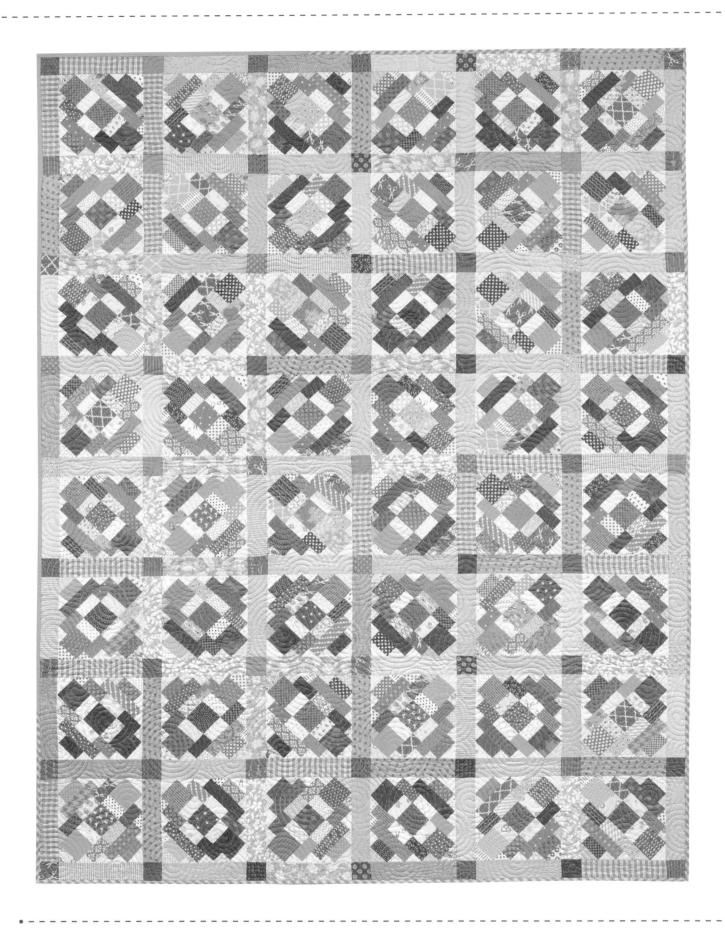

Lissa is a scrap-quilter extraordinaire, and her passion for scrappy is evident in nearly every quilt she makes. Visit ModaLissa.com.

- **A scrap that is** 2½" square is not too small for me to save. All my scraps get trimmed to either 1½" squares or 2½" squares.

- **In my dreams, the ideal scrappy quilt has at least** a gazillion different fabrics in it!

- **Let me tell you a little something about how I store my scraps.** I store all the 1½" squares together. All other sizes are stored by size and color.

- **When I start pulling fabrics for a scrappy quilt, I** begin with a multicolored piece of fabric. I look for something with colors I like the feel of overall. This piece usually isn't used in the scrap project, but it gives me confidence in pulling together the scraps.

- **If you look at my assortment of scraps, you'll see** low-volume (light) backgrounds are most prominent colors. **The color you'll find the least of in my scraps is** red, because I use it all up and have to buy yardage.

- **If I had a signature move, I'd say you'll know a quilt is mine by looking because** it would have a large mix of fabrics from Moda designers and my label quilted right into the quilt somewhere.

- **Thumbs up or thumbs down? Scrappy binding?** Thumbs down. **Scrappy backing?** Thumbs way up.

- **Here's my secret to keeping your ¼" seam allowances spot on:** Always use the same machine. This may seem odd, but a different machine, used at a class or retreat, will usually have a different ¼" foot.

Assembling the Blocks

1 Sew one red 3" x 42" strip between two light 2" x 42" strips. Press the seam allowances toward the red strip. Make five strip sets. Crosscut each strip set into 20 segments, 1¾" x 6", for a total of 96 A units (4 are extra).

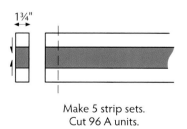

1¾"

Make 5 strip sets.
Cut 96 A units.

2 Sew one red 5½" x 42" strip between two light 2¼" x 42" strips. Press the seam allowances toward the red strip. Make five strip sets. Crosscut each strip set into 20 segments, 1¾" x 9", for a total of 96 B units (4 are extra).

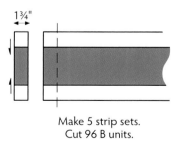

1¾"

Make 5 strip sets.
Cut 96 B units.

3 Join one light 3" x 42" strip, two red 3" x 42" strips, and two light 2" x 42" strips, alternating them as shown. Press the seam allowances toward the red strips. Make five strip sets. Crosscut each strip set into 20 segments, 1¾" x 11", for a total of 96 C units (4 are extra).

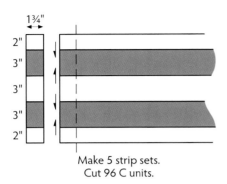

Make 5 strip sets.
Cut 96 C units.

4 Join three red 3" x 42" strips, two light 1¾" x 42" strips, and two light 2" x 42" strips, alternating them as shown. Make four strip sets. Crosscut each strip set into 13 segments, 3" x 13½", for a total of 48 D units (four are extra).

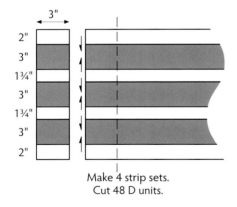

Make 4 strip sets.
Cut 48 D units.

5 Join two A units, two B units, two C units, one D unit, and two light 2" x 4" rectangles as shown, carefully matching the center points of all units. Press the seam allowances toward the D unit in the center.

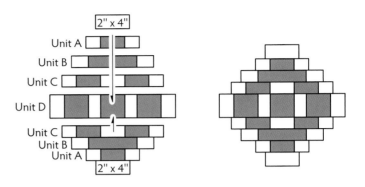

6 Trim the block to 9" square (which includes seam allowances), keeping the middle red square centered. Make 48 blocks.

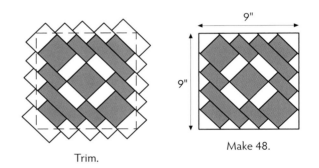

Trim.

Make 48.

Assembling the Quilt Top

1 Join one red 2½" x 42" strip and one gray 9" x 42" strip. Press the seam allowances toward the gray strip. Make four strip sets. Crosscut each strip set into 16 segments, 2½" x 11", for a total of 54 sashing units (10 are extra).

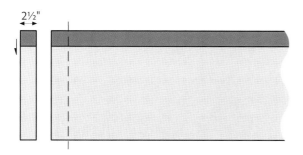

2½"

Make 4 strip sets.
Cut 54 segments.

Making a scrap quilt is the best way to gain color confidence. It's as if you're jumping off a cliff, but halfway down you grab a tree branch. Scrap quilts help you see value and scale, so the color choices become secondary in the project. Just have fun!

2 Join six sashing units and one red 2½" square as shown. Press the seam allowances toward the gray fabric. Make nine sashing rows. Join six blocks and seven gray 2½" x 9" rectangles as shown. Press the seam allowances toward the gray rectangles. Make eight block rows. Lay out and join the block and sashing rows as shown in the quilt assembly diagram below. Press the seam allowances toward the sashing rows.

Finishing the Quilt

For more details on quilting and finishing, go to ShopMartingale.com/HowtoQuilt.

1 Layer the backing, batting, and quilt top; baste the layers together. Hand or machine quilt as desired. The featured quilt was machine quilted with an allover spiral design.

2 Use the gray and red 2½"-wide binding strips to make and attach the binding. Lissa pieced the strips in sections of red and gray for a playful effect that enhances the scrappy look.

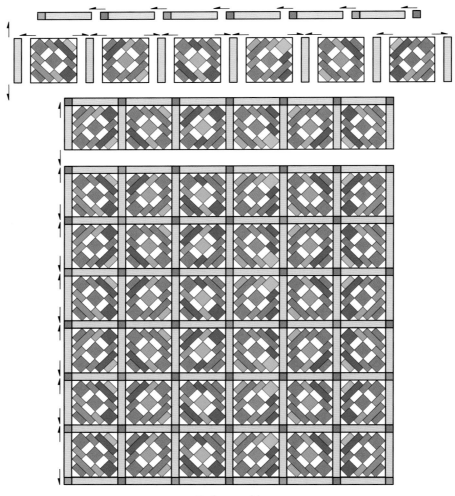

Quilt assembly

Designed by Lisa Calle; quilted by Lee Jenkins

Duck, Duck, Goose

Combine bright print scraps with a crisp navy and white color scheme to make the big and bold blocks for this striking quilt.

Finished quilt: 70½" x 88½"
Finished block: 16" x 16"

Materials

Yardage is based on 42"-wide fabric. Lisa used orange and blue scraps for 10 blocks and pink and green scraps for the other 10 blocks. Choose a color combination for the blocks in this manner, or mix and match print scraps randomly in each block for a scrappier look.

40 bright print 10" x 10" squares (10 *each* of blue, orange, pink and green) for blocks

40 bright print 5" x 5" squares (10 *each* of blue, orange, pink, and green) for blocks

3 yards of white solid for background

2⅔ yards of navy solid for blocks, sashing and binding

5½ yards of backing fabric

80" x 98" piece of batting

Cutting

All measurements include scant ¼"-wide seam allowances.

From the bright 10" squares, cut:
20 of the squares into 160 rectangles, 2½" x 4½"
20 of the squares into 320 squares, 2½" x 2½"

From the bright 5" squares, cut:
Each square into quarters diagonally to yield 160 triangles

From the white solid, cut:
20 strips, 2½" x 42"; crosscut into:
   160 rectangles, 2½" x 4½"
   12 squares, 2½" x 2½"
10 strips, 4⅞" x 42", crosscut into 80 squares, 4⅞" x 4⅞". Cut 40 of the squares in half diagonally to yield 80 triangles.

From the navy solid, cut:
5 strips, 4⅞" x 42"; crosscut into 40 squares, 4⅞" x 4⅞"
16 strips, 2½" x 42"; crosscut into 32 sashing strips, 2½" x 16½"
   (1 is extra)
9 strips, 2½" x 42"

Lisa is a four-star fabricologist when it comes to scrap quilts. She prefers a bit of order in her mix, but knows variety is still the spice! Visit LisaHCalle.com.

- **A scrap that is** 2" square is not too small for me to save. But only if I REALLY love the fabric!

- **In my dreams, the ideal scrappy quilt has at least** 50 different fabrics in it!

- **Let me tell you a little something about how I sort my scraps.** I sort by size and then by color.

- **When I start pulling fabrics for a scrappy quilt,** I begin with a general color palette. I like controlled scrappy, not everything in the rainbow, but a good variety.

- **If you look at my assortment of scraps, you'll see** green is the most prominent color. **The color you'll** find the least of in my scraps is purple. I just don't buy purple fabric.

- **The best advice I've received on choosing colors/ prints for scrap quilts was** to add a dark neutral to bring it all together. Black, navy, gray, and chocolate brown are good choices.

- **If I had a signature move, I'd say you'll know a quilt is mine by looking because** it is probably square and labeled!

- **Thumbs up or thumbs down? Scrappy binding?** THUMBS WAY UP! **Scrappy backing?** Yes, but only for quilts I'm keeping. Solid backs look nicer as gifts.

- **Here's my secret to keeping your ¼" seam allowances spot on:** A great ¼" foot!

Assembling the Block Units

1 Draw a diagonal line from corner to corner on the wrong side of the white 4⅞" squares. Place one white square right side together with one navy 4⅞" square. Stitch ¼" from each side of the drawn line. Cut along the drawn line to yield two half-square-triangle units. Press the seam allowances toward the navy fabric. Make 80 half-square-triangle units that measure 4½" square.

Make 80.

2 Draw a diagonal line from corner to corner on the wrong side of the bright 2½" squares. Place one marked bright square on one end of a white 2½" x 4½" rectangle as shown. Sew on the marked line. Trim the seam allowance to ¼" and press the square away from the rectangle. Repeat to sew a second marked bright square (same color but different print) to the opposite end of the rectangle. Make 160 flying-geese units that are 2½" x 4½".

Make 160.

3 Using a scant seam allowance, join two bright 5" triangles (blue and orange or pink and green) along one of the short edges. Press the seam allowances toward the darker fabric. Again using a scant seam allowance, sew a white triangle to the long edge of the unit as shown. Press the seam allowance toward the print triangles. Trim the unit to 4½" square. Make 80 half-hourglass units, always keeping the colors in the same position (i.e. orange on the left, blue on the right).

Make 80.

Assembling the Blocks

Each block is composed of four half-square-triangle units, eight flying-geese units, eight bright 2½" x 4½" rectangles, and four half-hourglass units. Assemble the blocks in quadrants. Choose all of the units for a block at once so that you have four flying-geese units of one color family and four of the other color family (pink and green or blue and orange). Choose the half-hourglass units to coordinate.

" *To create my quilt more accurately, press open the corner triangles and flying geese. It lets you see where the seam allowances should be meeting up.* "

1 Sew a flying-geese unit to a rectangle in the same color family, orienting the flying-geese points away from the rectangle. Press the seam allowances toward the rectangle. Make four of each colorway.

Make 4.   Make 4.

2 Sew one of the units from step 1 to a half-square-triangle unit as shown. Press the seam allowances toward the half-square-triangle unit. Sew the remaining unit from step 1 to a half-hourglass unit as shown. Join the two pieced units; press the seam allowances in one direction. Make four quadrants.

Make 4.

3 Lay out the quadrants in two rows of two as shown. Join the quadrants in each row; press the seam allowances in opposite directions. Join the rows; press the seam allowances in one direction. Make 20 blocks: 10 with blue and orange pieces and 10 using pink and green pieces. Each block should measure 16½" square, including seam allowances.

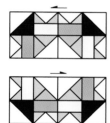 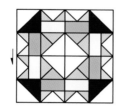

Make 20.

Assembling the Quilt Top

1 Lay out the blocks in five rows of four blocks each, alternating the colorways and positioning a navy sashing strip between the blocks in each row. Join the pieces in each row; press the seam allowances toward the sashing.

2 Join four sashing strips and three white 2½" squares as shown to make a sashing row. Make four sashing rows. Lay out the sashing rows between the block rows as shown, matching the seams. Join the block and sashing rows; press the seam allowances toward the sashing rows.

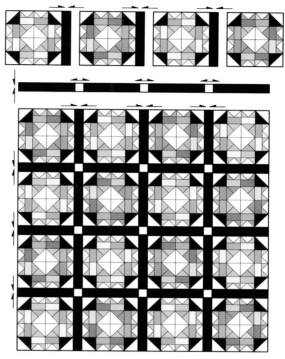

Quilt assembly

Finishing the Quilt

For more details on quilting and finishing, go to ShopMartingale.com/HowtoQuilt.

1 Layer the backing, batting, and quilt top; baste the layers together. Hand or machine quilt as desired. The featured quilt was machine quilted with a variety of motifs to highlight the shapes; a flower was quilted in each center square and cornerstone, and continuous curved lines were quilted in the navy triangles and sashing.

2 Use the remaining navy 2½"-wide strips to make and attach the binding.

Designed by Lynne Hagmeier; pieced by Lois Sprecker; quilted by Joy Johnson

Cutting Corners

Use precut strips to make this fun graphic block with a Churn Dash design in the center. A timesaving layered-patchwork technique lets you easily add the triangle pieces.

Finished quilt: 76" x 90"
Finished block: 14" x 14"

Materials

Yardage is based on 42"-wide fabric.

32 light strips, 2½" x 42", for blocks

32 dark strips, 2½" x 42", for blocks

1¼ yards of tan print for inner border

2½ yards of black print for outer border and binding

6 yards of backing fabric

82" x 96" piece of batting

Cutting

All measurements include scant ¼"-wide seam allowances. The quilt is composed of 10 dark blocks (A) and 10 light blocks (B). Plan the print combinations and group the pieces for each block before you begin sewing and refer to the quilt photo (page 85) for guidance if needed.

Cutting for 1 Block A

From the light strips, cut:
5 squares, 2½" x 2½"; cut *4 of the squares* in half diagonally to yield 8 triangles
2 rectangles, 2½" x 10½"
2 rectangles, 2½" x 14½"

From the dark strips, cut:
10 squares, 2½" x 2½"; cut *2 of the squares* in half diagonally to yield 4 triangles
2 rectangles, 2½" x 6½"
2 rectangles, 2½" x 10½"

Cutting for 1 Block B

From the light strips, cut:
10 squares, 2½" x 2½"; cut *2 of the squares* in half diagonally to yield 4 triangles
2 rectangles, 2½" x 6½"
2 rectangles, 2½" x 10½"

Continued on page 86

SCRAPS OF *Wisdom*
FROM LYNNE HAGMEIER

Lynne is a mighty mixologist when it comes to pulling together fabrics for her scrappy sensations. It helps that she designs many of the fabrics too! Visit KTQuilts.com.

- **A scrap that is** 2" square is not too small to save.

- **In my dreams, the ideal scrappy quilt has at least** a billion different fabrics in it. (You said to dream!)

- **Let me tell you a little something about how I store my scraps.** I have bins for each of my leftover precuts—mini charms, charms, Jelly Rolls, etc. Pieces smaller than fat-quarter sized are stored in locker baskets by color. Fat quarters or larger are stacked by color on shelves.

- **When I start pulling fabrics for a scrappy quilt,** I begin with a little bit of everything and edit as I sew.

- **If you look at my assortment of scraps, you'll see** red is the most prominent color. **The color you'll find the least of in my scraps is** pink.

- **The best advice I've received on choosing colors/ prints for scrap quilts was** if you love it, it will all go together.

- **If I had a signature move, I'd say you'll know a quilt is mine by looking because** it has layered patchwork blocks that softly fray when washed.

- **Thumbs up or thumbs down? Scrappy binding?** Thumbs up. **Scrappy backing?** I love it when I have the time.

- **Here's my secret to keeping your ¼" seam allowances spot on:** Use your ¼" foot and practice, practice, practice.

Continued from page 84

From the dark strips, cut:

5 squares, 2½" x 2½"; cut *4 of the squares* in half diagonally to yield 8 triangles

2 rectangles, 2½" x 10½"

2 rectangles, 2½" x 14½"

Cutting for Sashing, Borders, and Binding

From the light strips, cut:

10 squares, 2½" x 2½"; cut in half diagonally to yield 20 triangles

From the dark strips, cut:

10 squares, 2½" x 2½"; cut in half diagonally to yield 20 triangles

From the tan print, cut:

18 *lengthwise* strips, 4½" x 14½"

4 squares, 4½" x 4½"

From the black print, cut:

4 *lengthwise* strips, 6½" x 80"

4 *lengthwise* strips, 2½" x 80"

1 strip, 2½" x 42"

Assembling Block A

1 Place a light triangle on a dark 2½" square, *both* right sides up, and align the edges; pin. Stitch ⅛" from the triangle's diagonal raw edge using matching thread. (This layered-patchwork technique leaves a raw edge.) Don't trim the dark square behind the triangle. Make four.

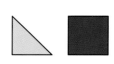

⅛"

Make 4.

2 Lay out the four layered squares with four dark 2½" squares and one light 2½" square in three rows of three as shown. Join the pieces in each row; press the seam allowances toward the dark squares. Join the rows to make a unit that is 6½" square, including the seam allowances. Press the seam allowances away from the center.

3 Sew dark 2½" x 6½" rectangles to the sides of the center unit; press the seam allowances toward the strips. Sew dark 2½" x 10½" rectangles to the top and bottom of the unit; press. The unit should be 10½" square.

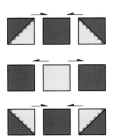
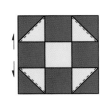

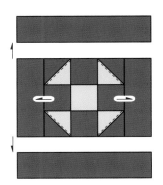

Any vintage basket, bin, or box is a worthy purchase if fabric can be stored in it.

4 Place four light triangles right side up on the corners of the unit, orienting them as shown; pin. Stitch ⅛" from the raw edges in the same manner as the triangles in step 1. Sew light 2½" x 10½" rectangles to the sides of the unit; press the seam allowances toward the strips just added. Sew light 2½" x 14½" rectangles to the top and bottom of the unit; press.

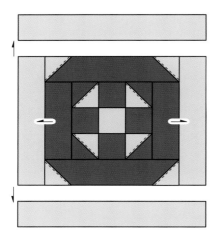

5 Layer and sew the remaining four dark triangles on the corners of the block using the same method for the previous triangles. Make 10 of block A. Blocks should measure 14½" square.

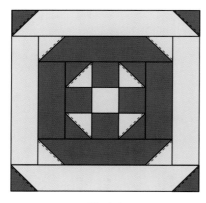

Block A.
Make 10.

6 Construct 10 of block B in the same manner as block A, reversing the dark and light placement.

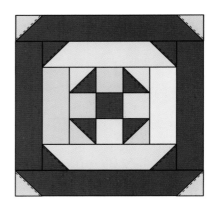

Block B.
Make 10.

Assembling the Quilt Top

1 Lay out five rows of four blocks, alternating the A and B blocks as shown in the quilt assembly diagram on page 89. Join the blocks in each row; press the seam allowances in alternating directions from row to row. Join the rows; press the seam allowances in one direction.

2 Place dark triangles on the lower corners of nine tan 4½" x 14½" strips with right sides facing up. Stitch ⅛" from the triangle edges. Repeat to stitch light triangles to the lower corners of nine tan strips. Stitch dark triangles to two tan 4½"squares and light triangles to two tan 4½"squares as shown.

Make 9.

Make 9.

Make 2.   Make 2.

3 Lay out the border strips and squares around the quilt-top perimeter as shown below, aligning light-triangle corners with dark-triangle corners and vice versa. Join the side border strips end to end; press the seam allowances in one direction. Sew the side borders to the quilt top; press the seam allowances toward the border strips. Join the top and bottom strips and corner squares. Sew the top and bottom borders to the top and bottom of the quilt; press.

4 Measure the quilt top vertically through the center. Trim two 6½"-wide black strips to the measurement, and then sew them to the sides of the quilt; press. Measure the quilt top horizontally through the center, and then trim and sew the black top and bottom borders in the same manner.

Finishing the Quilt

For more details on quilting and finishing, go to ShopMartingale.com/HowtoQuilt.

1 Layer the backing, batting, and quilt top; baste the layers together. Hand or machine quilt as desired. The featured quilt was machine quilted in the ditch between the blocks and borders, and then feathers and cross-hatching were added to highlight different sections of the block. The inner border was quilted with parallel lines spaced 2" apart.

2 Use the black 2½"-wide strips to make and attach the binding.

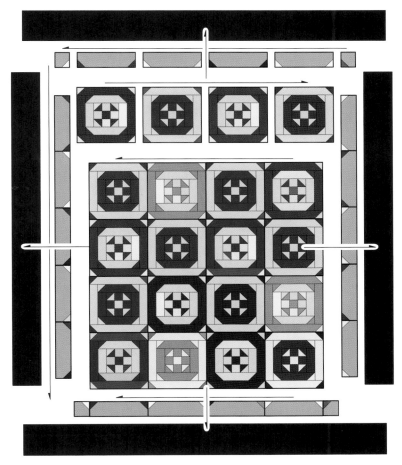

Quilt assembly

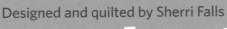

On the Grid

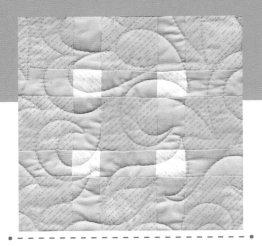

Cute grid-style blocks are a snap to cut and sew from precut strips and charm squares. Add a unique touch by framing the blocks with a pretty pieced border.

Finished quilt: 60" x 90"

Finished block: 8" x 8"

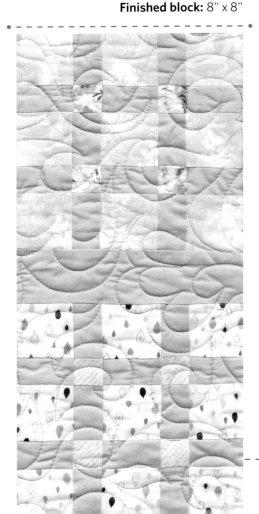

Materials

Yardage is based on 42"-wide fabric.

40 bright strips, 2½" x 42", for blocks

40 bright squares, 5" x 5", for blocks

4¾ yards of gray solid for block backgrounds

¾ yard of green floral for binding

5½ yards of backing fabric

66" x 96" piece of batting

Cutting

All measurements include scant ¼"-wide seam allowances.

From *each* bright strip, cut:

3 rectangles, 2½" x 9" (120 total)

From the remainders of the bright strips, cut a *total* of:

32 rectangles, 2½" x 8½"

4 rectangles, 2½" x 5½"

From *each* bright square, cut:

2 rectangles, 1½" x 4" (80 total)

From the gray solid, cut:

4 strips, 9" x 42"; crosscut into 80 rectangles, 1½" x 9"

2 strips, 8½" x 42"; crosscut into 32 rectangles, 2½" x 8½"

8 strips, 4" x 42"; crosscut into 120 rectangles, 2½" x 4"

28 strips, 2½" x 42"; crosscut *4 of the strips* into 64 squares, 2½" x 2½"

From the green floral, cut:

9 strips, 2½" x 42"

SCRAPS OF
Wisdom
FROM SHERRI FALLS

Sherri is a professional scraptender who sees the potential in all those bits and pieces of leftover fabric. Visit ThisAndThatPatterns.typepad.com.

- **A scrap that is** 2" square is not too small to save.

- **In my dreams, the ideal scrappy quilt has at least** 40 different fabrics in it, just like a Jelly Roll, Charm Pack, or Layer Cake does!

- **Let me tell you a little something about how I store my scraps.** I cut them into workable sizes such as 2½" squares, 4½"squares, and 2½" x 4½" rectangles, so they are ready for quilt projects when needed. I also like to cut scraps into 2½" by the width of fabric strips for strip projects or scrappy bindings.

- **When I start pulling fabrics for a scrappy quilt,** I begin with the main/focus fabric. It may be the border fabric, as I like to use larger prints for the border and smaller prints for the piecing so my quilt doesn't get too busy.

- **If you look at my assortment of scraps, you'll see** red is the most prominent color. **The color you'll find the least of in my scraps is** brown.

- **If I had a signature move, I'd say you'll know a quilt is mine by looking because** it most likely has red in it with a fun and whimsical look!

- **Thumbs up or thumbs down? Scrappy binding?** Sometimes. **Scrappy backing?** Thumbs up!

- **Here's my secret to keeping your ¼" seam allowances spot on:** Know your machine. Each one is different. I make sure the ¼" foot is accurate, or I mark the bed of the machine with cute washi tape as my guide.

Assembling the Blocks

1 Join three matching bright 2½" x 9" rectangles and two gray 1½" x 9" rectangles along the long edges as shown. Make 40 strip sets. Crosscut each strip set into three horizontal segments, 2½" x 8½", for a total of 120 segments.

2 Join three gray 2½" x 4" rectangles and two bright 1½" x 4" rectangles along the long edges as shown. Make 40 strip sets. Crosscut each strip set as shown to make two segments, 1½" x 8½", for a total of 80 segments.

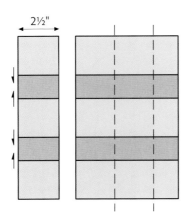

Make 40 strip sets.
Cut 120 segments.

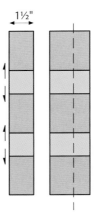

Make 40 strip sets.
Cut 80 segments.

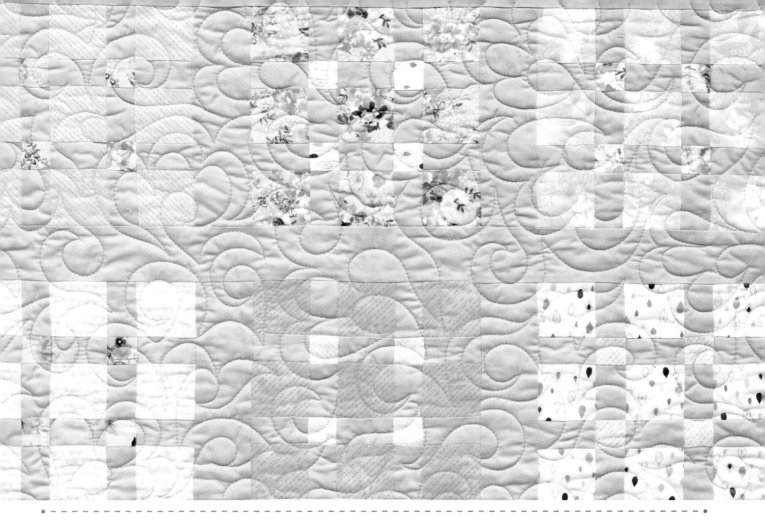

3 Lay out three matching large segments and two matching small segments as shown. Join the segments to complete the block. Press the seam allowances in one direction. Make 40 blocks, which measure 8½" square, including seam allowances.

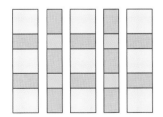 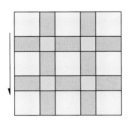

Make 40.

"*One tip that will make piecing my quilt more accurate is this: Be sure to PRESS, not iron, your strip segments so they stay straight.*"

Assembling the Quilt Top and Borders

1 Lay out eight rows of five blocks and four gray 2½" x 8½" rectangles. Join the blocks and rectangles in each row.

2 Join nine gray 2½" x 42" strips end to end. Crosscut the long strip into seven sashing strips, 2½" x 48½". Lay out the sashing strips between the block rows. Join the block rows and sashing strips; press the seam allowances toward the sashing strips.

3 Join seven gray 2½" x 42" strips end to end. Crosscut the strip unit into two long sashing strips, 2½" x 78½" and two short sashing strips, 2½" x 52½". Sew the long strips to the side of the quilt top; press the seam allowances toward the strips. Sew the short strips to the top and bottom of the quilt top; press.

4 Draw a diagonal line from corner to corner on the wrong side of the 64 gray 2½" squares. Place one marked square on one end of a bright 2½" x 8½" rectangle, right sides together. Sew on the drawn line. Trim the seam allowances to ¼", and then press the square away from the rectangle. Repeat to sew a gray square to the opposite end of the rectangle. Make 28 border units.

Make 28.

5 Sew marked gray squares to two bright 2½" x 8½" rectangles as shown, making sure to make the angles mirror image. Repeat to make two of each for a total of four long corner units, each from a different bright print.

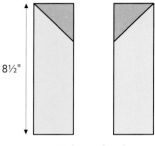

8½"

Make 2 of each.

6 Repeat step 4 using the bright 2½" x 5½" rectangles to make four short corner units, each from a different bright print.

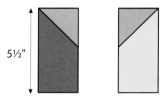

5½"

Make 2 of each.

7 Lay out nine border units and two short corner units along the sides of the quilt as shown in the quilt assembly diagram on page 95. Join the units; press the seam allowances in one direction. Sew the pieced borders to the sides of the quilt; press the seam allowances toward the quilt center. Lay out five border units and two long corner units along the top and bottom of the quilt center as shown. Join the units, and then sew them to the top and bottom of the quilt; press.

8 Join the eight remaining gray 2½" x 42" strips end to end. Crosscut the strip into two long outer borders, 2½" x 86½", and two short borders, 2½" x 60½". Sew the long outer borders to the sides of the quilt; press the seam allowances toward the outer borders. Sew the short outer borders to the top and bottom of the quilt; press.

Finishing the Quilt

For more details on quilting and finishing, go to ShopMartingale.com/HowtoQuilt.

1 Layer the backing, batting, and quilt top; baste the layers together. Hand or machine quilt as desired. The featured quilt was machine quilted with an allover swirl and feather design.

2 Join the green-floral 2½"-wide strips to make and attach the binding.

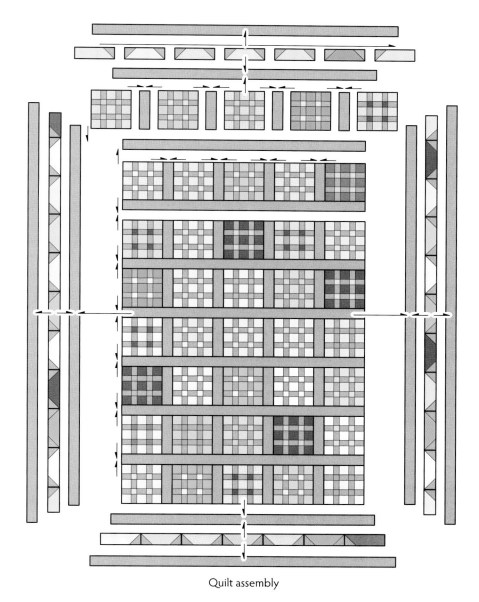

Quilt assembly

Meet the Moda All-Stars

Left to right: Laura Boehnke, Lisa Bongean, Corey Yoder, Sherri McConnell, Lynne Hagmeier, Jenny Doan, and Lissa Alexander

Here are just a few of the all-star designers whose quilts are featured in this book. For even more all-star fun, pick up a copy of *Moda All-Stars All in a Row.*

What's your creative passion?

Find it at **ShopMartingale.com**

books • eBooks • ePatterns • daily blog • free projects
videos • tutorials • inspiration • giveaways

Create with Confidence